First published 1999 by Cornell University Press

Printed in the United States of America

A volume in the Cornell Studies in Security Affairs series, edited by Robert J. Art, Robert Jervis, and Stephen M. Walt.

LIBRARY OF CONGRESS CATALOGUING-IN-PUBLICATION DATA
Neustadt, Richard E.
    Report to JFK : the Skybolt crisis in perspective / Richard E.
Neustadt.
        p. cm.
    Includes index.
    ISBN 0-8014-3622-2
    1. United States—Foreign relations—Great Britain case studies.
    2. Great Britain—Foreign relations—United States case studies.
    3. United States—Foreign relations—1961–1963—Decision making
case studies.   4. Strategic weapons systems—United States—History—
20th century.   5. Kennedy, John F. (John Fitzgerald), 1917–1963.
    6. Macmillan, Harold, 1894– .   I. Title.
    E183.8.G7N474   1999
    327.73041—dc21   99-23992

Cornell University Press strives to use environmentally responsible suppliers and materials to the fullest extent possible in the publishing of its books. Such materials include vegetable-based, low-VOC inks and acid-free papers that are recycled, totally chlorine-free, or partly composed of nonwood fibers. Books that bear the logo of the FSC (Forest Stewardship Council) use paper taken from forests that have been inspected and certified as meeting the highest standards for environmental and social responsibility. For further information, visit our website at www.cornellpress.cornell.edu.

Cloth printing   10 9 8 7 6 5 4 3 2 1

FSC FSC Trademark © 1996 Forest Stewardship Council A.C.
    SW-COC-098

Contents

Report to JFK

1

Introduction

In December 1962, the President of the United States, John F. Kennedy, received an unpleasant surprise. Three months after the Cuban missile crisis, just as he was ready for a relaxed Christmas season, he found himself facing an unexpected crisis of confidence with his country's closest ally, the United Kingdom.

Kennedy faced it literally, across the table from the Prime Minister, Harold Macmillan, at Nassau, the Bahamas, then still a British possession. Their meeting had been scheduled long since for December 19–21, as one among a series of pleasant periodic get-togethers. It turned out to be a tense and, on the British side, distinctly angry confrontation over American cancellation of the Skybolt missile. This confrontation Kennedy had anticipated for only a week.

Skybolt was an air-to-surface weapon, still in development, on which Britain had relied to prolong life for its manned bombers, then its sole strategic nuclear deterrent. Macmillan insisted on Polaris, the first submarine-to-surface missile, as his seaborne substitute. In the event, Kennedy conceded, which was more than most of his advisers thought he should have done. His course seemed the more questionable in January 1963, when President Charles de Gaulle of France vetoed British entry into the European Economic Community—as the European Union then was styled—using the Nassau agreement for his symbol and excuse: Britain's insufficient Europeanness and the transatlantic entanglements of its deterrent.

So, early in 1963, Kennedy was in the mood for a postmortem.

By coincidence, just then I had approached his Special Assistant for National Security Affairs, McGeorge Bundy, seeking privileged access to the documentation on that crisis with the British, because I wished to use it as the first in a series of case studies on alliance relations. Back came the word that the President felt he could not sanction anything for publication but was contemplating an in-house review. I replied, at once, that I would gladly trade publicity for knowledge and offered to do it. The offer was promptly accepted. It was formalized in a brief memo from JFK, followed by a seventeen-minute conversation in mid-April, when he told me what he wanted.

That memo, concocted by Carl Kaysen, Bundy's deputy, and me, is reproduced at the end of this chapter. I made multiple copies and carried them everywhere, each serving as an open sesame, even in England (to the extent described below).

Seven months later, I submitted my report, titled "Skybolt and Nassau: American Policy-Making and Anglo-American Relations." Kennedy read it November 17. Five days more, and he was dead; it became part of his estate. Almost thirty years after that, it was declassified and released.[1] This book makes it available for general use. I always thought it an illuminating case study and hope it serves students as such.

The report itself is contained in Chapter 2. Chapter 3 reviews the report by light of what the British files disclose. They too were made public after thirty years, and I have been through them for the purpose. Chapter 4 reprints a paper I sketched in 1964 and redrafted the next year for presentation to the American Political Science Association. It characterizes and compares the two governments as they were at roughly the time of the Skybolt affair. Chapter 5 brings that comparison up to date. A glossary of obscure terms and a cast of characters for 1962 round out this Introduction.

To return to the history of the report as such, it was easy for me to offer an "in-house" study and for Kennedy to accept, because I had been from the start of his Administration a consultant to the President and the Budget Director on matters they, or White House aides, chose to refer to me in spheres organizational and operational (general enough to cover this project comfortably), with appropriate security clearances.

Indeed, I had held that status since before the Administration's start. On a dull news day late in 1960, I had been publicly announced as "Special Consultant to the President-Elect"—a fancy designation for ad hoc assistance—and had worked actively on organizational questions until after the Inaugural. Through a series of happy accidents, I had first met Kennedy that September. I was introduced to him as a knowledgeable former White House aide to the most recent Democratic President, Harry S Truman. Kennedy, then running hard, had asked me for some memoranda on transition, just in case. I had done them, been thanked publicly as well as privately, and then been kept on hand in those consultative roles.

These things I note because they guaranteed my bona fides with the whole of Washington, when, two years later, I set out to reconstruct the Skybolt story. The Cabinet members had encountered me before they themselves took office, and their officials knew me or had read about me.

What JFK said he wanted from that reconstruction, when I saw him on April 27, 1963, was an understanding of precisely what had happened on his side of the Atlantic, at every governmental level from bottom to top, his own included, to occasion his surprise the previous December and his felt need to assist Macmillan—and also what had happened on the British side to the extent I could find out. This, Kennedy made plain, was in the interest of the future, of utility to him in learning lessons for the future, not an abstract interest in the history per se, though I don't doubt he felt that too.

In 1963 I was teaching at Columbia University, with perhaps a day a week in Washington. I increased that to three days, at pain to my family, spending April and most of May reading my way into the story through everyone's files. I began with Bundy's, then proceeded to those of several involved officials at Defense and State. Nowhere did I present my purpose as seeking to find fault—why should I? it wasn't—but rather to find lessons useful for the President. Everyone naturally treasured some of what they thought were such lessons, and as a first step in educating me, so that I could educate him, opened their files with a will. Nowhere in Washington did I encounter any appearance of concern, reluctance, or evasion. So far as I could tell, my bona fides held firm.

I especially recall one senior State official who cheerfully lent me his whole chronological file for 1961–63 (to date), where I read instance after instance of induced reporting on many things other than Skybolt (mainly on the Multilateral Force, of which more later). He continuously asked friends at various American embassies abroad to see if they could not find in the foreign government, and then report to Washington, sentiments he wished his associates there to discover. Usually his friends reported what he wanted. As an innocent former White House aide, I was shocked! But there decidedly were lessons to be learned, and he was unselfconscious about teaching them.

By late May 1963, I thought I had absorbed enough to begin interviewing participants in the Skybolt crisis and its antecedents. I did so. Everyone was cooperative, and generous to a fault with time. I listened carefully and always sympathetically, as I had learned to do the hard way, in previous research. The month of June was spent full-time in Washington, as were the first weeks of July. The President was then in Europe, where I did not wish to be until his return—so that my historical questions could not be confused in any way with current policy. Once he was back in the United States, I set off to tackle London.

My interview notes with major participants in both cities were converted at the time to finished memoranda of conversations (in case Kennedy wished to see them), marked "sensitive," not a security classification, and kept by me all these years in a file drawer. I will dispatch them now to the Kennedy Library in Boston. Rough, handwritten notes for these, and also of my interviews with other persons, wereplaced there long ago, although many remain classified and some seem to be missing. Fortunately, all the attributed quotations in my report are covered by the memcons. For present readers I have noted their dates (as I did not for Kennedy).[2] Anyone who wishes will be able to pursue them at the Library.

The then British Ambassador to Washington, Sir David Ormsby Gore, later Lord Harlech, who had been friendly with the President since before the Second World War, knew all about my project and already had been interviewed, as one among the Washingtonians. I asked him how I should approach his government. For reasons best known to himself, he replied "unofficially." I did not understand his reasons then but did not question them. (Now, having read the British files, I think he was ducking, not casually.)[3] So off I went to the U.K., via Paris where NATO then was headquartered, to see what I could do through friends of friends, arranging unofficially for comparable interviews.

During the fifteen months before September 1962, I had lived in England, to my family's delight, on sabbatic leave from Columbia, lecturing at Nuffield College, Oxford. I had used the time, in part, as a sort of busman's holiday, wandering around Westminster and Whitehall, meeting politicians, officials, and journalists, seeking to grasp all I could about the workings of their system. Thus, when I returned to London ten months later, I had plenty of friends to phone. My first step was to call on our Ambassador, the wise and charming David Bruce, whom I had known somewhat ever since President Truman's time. Bruce, hearing my tale, volunteered a desk and telephone. Thereupon I called my friends, they theirs, and so forth, until I had lined up six interviews, all but one with incumbent ministers or officials. To me (and to Bruce) that seemed a good start.

The next day, one by one, within the space of two hours, five of those interviews were politely canceled. I was left with Harold Watkinson, the former Defence Minister, who had been out of office since July 1962! (I did see him, of course.) Taking pity on me, Bruce arranged that I should wait upon the Permanent Under-Secretary at the Foreign Office, then Sir Harold Caccia. To Caccia I gave a copy of my memo from JFK. He brightened up at once, noting that it said nothing about Skybolt per se. He then explained that the Prime Minister, having heard about my visit and its purpose, had objected to anyone's discussing Skybolt with strange foreigners, especially professors, who probably were journalists in disguise. The FO had already asked Gore about me and would now take his affirmative response, together with the memo, back to Macmillan.

So Caccia did (quite elaborately, their record now has shown me). This I discovered the next morning, when my five lost interviews were courteously restored, again by phone calls, one after the other, along with a couple more that I hadn't yet dared attempt.

Bruce was pleased, I relieved, and I went about my business assiduously for the next three weeks, interviewing everyone I wished, except Macmillan. Initial reserve waned when I appeared at once informed and sympathetic, and as my interviewees, seemingly, came to believe that—strange or not—I really was intent upon reporting only to the President. In the end, I think, those Londoners were as helpful and forthcoming as the Washingtonians (although the memcons in their own files are far less informative than those in mine, which amounts to self-protection, I suppose).

Then, after a family vacation, I returned to the United States, knowing all I could hope to learn, since British files were closed for twenty-nine more years, and thus confronted with the daunting task of writing my report. I had already decided to do the work in Washington, because my files were secured there and cleared secretarial assistance was available there, not at Columbia. So, when the university term commenced I resumed my three-day-a-week stint and wrote in a room at the Old Executive Office Building. It took me until the end of the first week in November. The finished product went across the street to Kennedy only on November 15, 1963. I did not know that I was almost out of time.

The report took so long to write because I had decided that to get it read I would have to beat James Bond (more precisely Ian Fleming). The President wished to learn lessons, but a report in managerial style, listing them for him directly, would not, I feared, be competitive. Instead, I decided I must tell the story, vividly and with suspense, letting the lessons emerge naturally from it, confining my own commentary to a coda at the end. Since that was not, for me, a native art form I was slow about it.

But I did succeed in my literary objective, that much I know. The President read the report by the pool at his family's house in Palm Beach, on Sunday, November 17. He then gave it to his wife, as she told me months later, remarking, "If you want to know what my life is like, read this." She said it was the first government document he'd ever given her, and she was so struck by this that she kept it with her, trying to read in snatches during their trip to Texas that same week. Kennedy also phoned Bundy in Washington, as I learned later, said he wished to see me once he was back there, after Thanksgiving, and gave a remarkable instruction:

Bundy was to phone Gore, have him come to the White House, read the second copy of the report (which I had providentially provided), and let Kennedy know whether, in Gore's opinion, the President could send it to Macmillan—recently retired—as a Christmas present. Considering that I had dutifully stamped it TOP SECRET NO FORN (meaning no foreigners), because it quoted documents then so classified, I have always thought this positively princely. Gore indeed came in, on the Wednesday, he later told me, read the report and left "yes" as his reply. But Kennedy didn't live to send it; he was shot in Dallas on the Friday.

Nor did I see him, one of the regrets of my life. The report then passed into his papers. With difficulty it was declassified, twenty-nine years and five months later, by the National Security Council staff, which had assumed jurisdiction.

Have I other regrets? At least two: I wish I could have had access to British records at the time. As Chapter 3 shows, they would have offered JFK a richer, still more entertaining story. And I wish that my conclusion had been kinder to Harold Wilson. In the event, during his Premiership, his pro-Americanism was every bit as sturdy as Macmillan's. Perhaps more so: Macmillan did not have to evade Lyndon Johnson's war, yet try to help us out of it, or put up with the latter's thinly veiled contempt.

In retrospect, one thing strikes me as curious about my months on the Skybolt assignment: While the project puzzled the British, it did not seem to puzzle the Americans. That JFK wished to draw lessons from his own experience, that he should enlist a professor to tease them out for him, and that he should be left alone to read (or not) what the professor wrote at his sole discretion appeared natural, so far as I could tell, to everyone on our side of the ocean. That is a tribute to Kennedy, or to the times, or both. One scarcely can imagine it in the circumstances of today.

Among all those I interviewed, there was but one who sought to read my report after the President's death. That was Robert McNamara, Secretary of Defense, who deviled a copy out of JFK's executor, Robert Kennedy. McNamara read it and we subsequently discussed it. He had but one point of difference with it. I had written that in August 1962 he concluded Skybolt should go, but the time for announcement was not yet. No, McNamara told me, that was not the way he thought about things. Rather, his August thought would have been, if, by November, circumstances remained unchanged from August, then he would conclude that it should go. The difference is subtle but not insignificant. I gladly note it now.

What of the press? Did no one know what I was up to all those months?

My memory is shadowed on the subject, but I think the answer has to be that many knew—since I then had friends galore in Washington's press corps—but all assumed that if the President wished a private study done, for his own edification, that was his right, provided I in my turn was discreet. I was. Nobody probed.

Henry Brandon, correspondent of the London *Sunday Times*, who was indeed a friend, did let me know that he planned feature stories on the Skybolt controversy for its first anniversary in December 1963. Thereupon, we meticulously agreed not to discuss our several researches and didn't, except for a few bits of color, not substance. Nor did he even hint at seeking to read my report. Years later I was grateful to him for his features, which were generally quite accurate on top-level behavior (he did not try to penetrate below), when I had to re-research Skybolt from public sources before publishing *Alliance Politics*. At the time I was annoyed for both of us when I had to write letters to London denying Opposition allegations that Brandon's reportage was based on mine.

Again, could such things happen now? I ask, not knowing.

What Kennedy made of my report there is no means to tell, beyond the fragments mentioned above. What he might have done with it, Macmillan aside, is equally unclear. I had some notions, but they did not extend beyond a reading by, and frank talk with, the Secretaries of State and Defense. I hoped they could be brought into agreement on the absolute importance of timely debriefing. I hoped he'd been persuaded of, and would avow to them, the dangers in more subtle, halfway stances than our blunt bureaucracies could implement without distortion and a plethora of "hunting licenses." I hoped they could agree upon the further dangers of neglecting to consider friends with the same care as enemies. Regarding dangers of both sorts, I speculated on some applications to Vietnam, beyond my bailiwick. I even hoped that with my mirror held before them, he and Rusk could grow more comfortable with each other. How the President might have reacted to such hopes, had we met and I voiced them as I planned, I cannot say, except that reportedly, in their Sunday phone call he commented to Bundy, "I don't know who the hell I can show this to"—apart, of course, from Macmillan, his fellow chief-of-government.

So the report remains what it was on November 15, 1963, written for a single reader. Given the opportunity, I would do it again.

POSSIBLY OBSCURE REFERENCES

Chapter 2 contains numbers of acronyms and other brief references that would have been familiar to President Kennedy, but may be obscure to readers now. I have assembled all I have noticed, and define them here so that the puzzled reader has one place to look for enlightenment. If there is no puzzlement, so much the better; no need to look.

A-3. The then most advanced model of the Polaris missile, still in development, which Macmillan, at Nassau, successfully insisted Britain be allowed to purchase.

Admiralty House. The Prime Minister's temporary quarters in Whitehall, while 10 Downing Street was under repair.

Admiral (George) Anderson. The U.S. Chief of Naval Operations who reportedly threw Secretary McNamara out of his headquarters at one point during the Cuban missile crisis. Shortly after, the Admiral was retired, and sent as Ambassador to Portugal, a former naval power.

ANF. Atlantic Nuclear Force, a proposed British alternative to the MLF, which, alongside a mixed-manned force (if any) of missile-bearing surface ships assigned to NATO, would have contained nationally manned sea- or airborne elements contributed from particular allied countries (e.g., Britain).

Ann Arbor. The site of a controversial commencement address by the American Secretary of Defense, Robert S. McNamara, in May 1962, in which he deprecated national nuclear deterrents built by allies (as the French were then attempting and eventually succeeded in doing), in the interest of flexible response, centrally controlled. British protest caused him to announce that he hadn't mean them, since their deterrent was already targeted with the American.

Athens. The site of a closed NATO conference in December 1961, in which McNamara voiced the themes he would publicize at Ann Arbor five months later, without arousing particular protests.

BNA. The British North America "Desk" (Office) in the European Bureau of the U.S. State Department, which by long tradition included Canada.

"Chiefs" and "Indians." A once-popular American slang distinction between the topmost and all other ranks in government.

EUR. The Bureau of European Affairs in the American Department of State.

FO. The British Foreign & Commonwealth Office, as now styled, headed by the Foreign Secretary, a senior member of the Cabinet, and by its chief civil servant, the Permanent Under-Secretary.

Great George Street. Leading into Parliament Square; the location of the Treasury in London.

Green Book. The report of the study led by former Secretary of State Dean Acheson in the early months of 1961, which was given policy effect by NSAM 147.

Harriman Mission. In November 1962, when Chinese troops invaded northern India, Averell Harriman, then Assistant Secretary of State for Far Eastern Affairs and also a respected elder statesman, accompanied by Carl Kaysen, among others, flew to New Delhi to inquire into Indian needs for assistance with arms and funds.

HMG. Conventional British shorthand for "Her Majesty's Government."

Holy Loch. The Scottish base for U.S. Polaris submarines on which Eisenhower and Macmillan agreed in 1960—at some political risk to the latter—and announced from Camp David at the same time as their Skybolt agreement.

IANF. An American precursor of the British proposal for an ANF, coupling national nuclear components from the United States, the United Kingdom, and perhaps France to a mixed-manned MLF contributed by others.

ISA. Office of International Security Affairs, part of the Office of the U.S. Secretary of Defense, dealing with political and economic matters, including arms sales, beyond the purview of the uniformed services as such.

JCS. The American Joint Chiefs of Staff.

Katanga. The mineral-rich southern province of the former Belgian Congo, newly independent, which in 1962 was threatening to separate itself, a threat the British government deplored as destabilizing to the region and associated with the independence thrust of Ian Smith in neighboring Rhodesia.

Lend-Lease. The authorizing legislation and ensuing program, sponsored by Franklin D. Roosevelt, which between March 1941 and May 1945 sent munitions without monetary compensation to the British, Soviets, and lesser allies fighting against Hitler.

"Macmillan's Purge." The not-so-routine shake-up of the Cabinet in July 1962, when seven members were dismissed all at once.

Merchant Mission. A group of officials under Livingston Merchant—very senior in the U.S. Foreign Service—sent by the American State Department to other NATO governments in February 1963, ostensibly to explore their interest, if any, in pursuing the idea of MLF. The group was so large, however, traveled in such style, and was treated with such deference by American ambassadors as to be criticized for leaving the impression that MLF was what Washington wanted. This ran beyond Kennedy's intention, though not beyond that of enthusiasts inside the Department.

MLF. Multilateral Force. A proposed seaborne force, subordinate to NATO, which would constitute an additional nuclear arm for the alliance. Members could contribute funds and personnel for mixed-manned ships firing nuclear-tipped missiles, with each contributor having a veto on their use. Submarines were initially envisaged, then surface freighters. Thus German funds and sailors could obtain a nuclear role without allowing their country to possess national nuclear weapons. Avoiding those for Germans, despite British weaponry and French ambitions, was the underlying purpose of it all, the outgrowth of a summer study in 1960, led by Robert Bowie. Whether Bonn would otherwise develop such ambitions remained in dispute.

MOD. The British Ministry of Defence, under the Secretary of State for Defence, invariably a Cabinet member (often referred to, informally, as Minister of Defence).

Monnet, Jean. A French writer and sometime official, fluent in English and persuasive in all languages, who was a mainspring of efforts toward European union in the decades after World War II. He was particularly associated with the Coal and Steel Community and then with the Common Market. As a member of the Free French Purchasing Commission in Washington during the war, Monnet had developed lasting friendships with Americans on Lend-Lease assignments, including George Ball, who was to become Kennedy's Undersecretary of State.

MRBM. Medium Range Ballistic Missile.

NAC. North Atlantic Council, the highest consultative body in NATO, including representatives of all member governments.

NSAM 147. A National Security Action Memorandum of April 1962, applying a previous report prepared under the guidance of Dean Acheson at Kennedy's invitation. It conveyed ideas about conventional rearmament, as well as nuclear integration, soon to be publicized at Ann Arbor, and came down against aid for a French independent nuclear force.

Porte Dauphine. The Paris location of NATO headquarters before its shift to Brussels.

Profumo case. A scandal from the spring of 1963, culminating that June, when a British minister had to resign after admitting that he had lied in and to the House of Commons about his personal conduct. Thereupon, Macmillan's government survived a vote of confidence despite more than forty abstentions on the Tory side.

PSAC. The President's Science Advisory Committee, a prestigious group surrounding the President's Science Adviser, created by President Eisenhower, abolished by President Nixon.

RAF. The Royal Air Force.

RAND. A "think tank," as we would now say, in Santa Monica, California, created at the start of the 1950s, initially with sustaining funds from the U.S. Air Force. RAND did pioneering work in bringing analytic techniques to strategic and operational problems in the national security sphere. Many of McNamara's "whiz kids" in the early 1960s came from there. RAND continues today with a more domestic emphasis and much more varied funding, and includes a notable graduate school.

Rhodesia. The British colony of Southern Rhodesia (now Zimbabwe) which in 1962, under a white-supremacist Premier, Ian Smith, declared independence, over the continuing opposition of the British government.

RS-70. The redesignation (as a reconnaissance strike aircraft) of the B-70, a bomber under development in Eisenhower's time. Despite its new guise, McNamara decided to cancel it in 1961, on grounds that by the time it was produced, Soviet defenses would render it excessively vulnerable. Having taken that decision after the recommended funding was already before Congress, the Administration had to fight hard with the weapon's friends on the Hill, Air Force of course included, to reverse the recommendation. This taught the Secretary of Defense and his Controller a lesson they applied in the Skybolt case.

SAC. The Strategic Air Command in the U.S. Air Force.

Spiegel affair. A media sensation in West Germany, shadowing with scandal the repute, and hence the electoral prospects, of the governing Christian Democrats.

USAF. The American Air Force.

Vassall case. A scandal from the fall of 1962, when J. W. C. Vassall, an Admiralty official, was discovered to be engaged in espionage for the Soviet Union. He was promptly tried and convicted, but there lingered allegations that a junior minister, Thomas Galbraith, was involved. This became a press and parliamentary issue, and was resolved, with Galbraith cleared, only in April 1963.

Wristonization. The process, named after the chair of the commission recommending it, by which the Departmental Service of the American State Department (which traditionally had filled most posts in Washington) was integrated into the Foreign Service (which had previously filled mostly foreign assignments). This was done in the mid-1950s under the secretaryship of John Foster Dulles.

CHAPTER 2'S CAST OF CHARACTERS

My report is full of names, almost all of which would have been familiar to President Kennedy in 1963. None can be presumed so to readers at the end of the century. Therefore, I have brought together here, in one place, alphabetically, brief identifications for them all, listing first the Americans, then the British since that is the order in which they mostly appear. Readers of Chapter 2 are invited to refer back to these lists as often as they find it useful to do so.

Americans in November 1962

Ball, George. Undersecretary of State (there then was no Deputy Secretary). A Washington lawyer with an international practice, wartime associate and convinced follower of Jean Monnet (the advocate of European Union), adviser to Adlai Stevenson in 1952, '56 and '60, Ball had come into the Kennedy Administration as Undersecretary for Economic Affairs; his focused energy, intelligence, and application already had won him a promotion.

Bell, David. Director of the Budget. An economist, former Secretary of Harvard's Graduate School of Public Administration, as it then was, and before that Administrative Assistant to President Truman, Bell was personable, thoughtful, analytic, and experienced.

Bohlen, Charles. One of the two top Russian specialists in the State Department, recently appointed Ambassador to France. More a thoroughly skilled operator than a deep analyst, Bohlen was bored in Paris, feeling out of things.

Bowie, Robert. A Harvard law professor, with force, focus, and charm, he had directed the Policy Planning staff at State under John Foster Dulles in Eisenhower's first term, then returned to Harvard as founding director of the Center for International Affairs, while remaining State's consultant. In these capacities he had headed the Summer Study of 1960 which fathered MLF.

Brown, Harold. Director of Defense Research and Engineering. A noted physicist, acute and operationally skillful, in McNamara's confidence. (Later to be President Carter's Secretary of Defense).

Bruce, David. Kennedy's Ambassador in London, having served Eisenhower so in Bonn and Paris, and Truman as Undersecretary of State under Dean Acheson. Bruce was charming, adroit, aging, a great stylist.

Bundy, McGeorge. Special Assistant to the President for National Security Affairs and, as such, head of the NSC staff (then still small). Formerly Dean of Arts and Sciences at Harvard at a young age, co-author of Henry Stimson's memoirs, "Mac" was bright, quick, confident, determined, striving to be the perfect staffman, juggling many balls at once.

Courtney, Raymond. Politico-Military Counselor at the American Embassy in London. Honorable, conscientious, experienced, not very imaginative.

Dillon, Douglas. Secretary of the Treasury. Previously Eisenhower's Undersecretary of State, and thus embodying "bipartisanship" as well as "fiscal responsibility," the legacy of earlier work on Wall Street. Dillon was engagingly direct, practical, experienced, disinclined to reach beyond his own (broad) departmental boundaries except on Kennedy's invitation.

Douglass, James. Eisenhower's last Deputy Secretary of Defense under Thomas Gates.

Enthoven, Alain. Director for Weapons Systems Analysis and Deputy to Charles Hitch, the Controller of the Defense Department. Along with Hitch, Enthoven was McNamara's leading "whiz kid," although brought to the Pentagon from RAND by Gates in 1959. A keen intelligence with rather blunt fingertips, not yet as sandpapered by experience as they later became.

Fessenden, Russell. Foy Kohler's Assistant at State in 1960, recently assigned overseas: sophisticated, knowledgeable, with sensitive fingertips, especially when once burned—but gone from Washington.

Gates, Thomas. Eisenhower's last Secretary of Defense, privy to the Camp David agreements in 1960, never hot for Skybolt, thoroughly cold before leaving office.

Gilpatric, Roswell. Deputy Secretary of Defense. Wall Street lawyer, skilled, sophisticated, broad-gauged, loyal to McNamara.

Hitch, Charles. Assistant Secretary of Defense and Controller. Former head of the Economics Division at RAND, previously an Oxford don, learned, experienced, intelligent, and tough; a natural fit of man and job.

Johnson, U. Alexis. Deputy Undersecretary of State. A senior career Foreign Service officer, most recently Ambassador to Thailand; successful in the Service in all senses of the phrase.

Kaysen, Carl. Deputy to Bundy at the White House and NSC. A professor of economics on leave from Harvard, Kaysen had worked up expertise in defense policy and weaponry, among other things: brilliant, subtle, confident, analytic but also a looker-around-corners.

Keeny, Spurgeon. Assistant to Jerome Wiesner (and part-time to Kaysen). A physicist with training in international relations, associated from its start in 1959 with the President's Science Adviser's Office, Keeny was personable, sophisticated, discreet, and a great quiet gatherer of bureaucratic intelligence.

Kitchen, Jeffrey. Director of the State Department Office of Politico-Military Affairs: medium brains, medium guts, good heart.

Kohler, Foy. William Tyler's predecessor as Assistant Secretary of State for European Affairs and as such involved in the Camp David agreements; recently posted abroad.

Legere, Colonel Laurence. Detailed to Bundy's office from the Joint Chiefs of Staff. A "military intellectual" but perhaps a bit out of his depth.

McNamara, Robert. Secretary of Defense. Recruited from the presidency of the Ford Motor Company, a driving, managing, no-nonsense—also no-pomposity—rationalist; his adherence to reason and duty was so passionate as to hint at emotion hidden beneath.

Nitze, Paul. Assistant Secretary of Defense for International Security Affairs. Experienced in defense and diplomacy since 1940, sophisticated, competent, cool, public cold warrior and private philanthropist, Nitze had all the skills and some of the limitations of the driving young banker he had once been.

Owen, Henry. Rostow's Deputy in the Policy Planning Council, as it was then named, at State. One of the two highest-ranking departmental civil servants not in the Foreign Service. Helpful, thoughtful, indefatigable; capable when roused of dedication bordering on fanaticism.

Rostow, Walt. Counselor to the State Department and Chairman of the Policy Planning Council, MIT economist, a driving enthusiast and conceptualizer with a tendency to listen to himself.

Rowen, Henry. Nitze's Deputy at International Security Affairs. A former RAND economist, and as such another "whiz kid," analytic, intelligent, rather new to Washington.

Rubel, John. Brown's Deputy at Defense Research and Engineering. An electrical engineer with four years on the job, indeed one of the few to hold the same job from before the 1960 Camp David meeting through the whole of 1962.

Rusk, Dean. Secretary of State. Experienced, thoughtful, conventional, perhaps essentially shy, temperamentally at odds with his presumed model and undoubted mentor, General Marshall, Rusk may never have felt at ease with JFK, to say nothing of articulate aides like Kaysen.

Schaetzel, Robert. Tyler's Deputy for European Regional Affairs at State, The other most senior civil servant not a Foreign Service officer, experienced, energetic, determined, a recent convert to Monnet's cause, and as such perhaps more holy than the Pope.

Taylor, General Maxwell. Chairman of the Joint Chiefs of Staff. New on the job, following a year at the White House as Military Adviser, he had come out of retirement after a distinguished career to support JFK in 1960: one person at the Pentagon the President knew well enough to trust.

Tyler, William. Assistant Secretary of State for European Affairs. Perhaps the most cultivated person in the department, deeply intelligent, basically shy, a bit mannered but beneath it shrewd and detached.

Weiss, Seymour. Kitchen's Deputy in Politico-Military Affairs. Another civil servant at State who was not a Foreign Service officer, but instead had a background at the Budget, among other places, "Sy" was energetic, straightforward, rather thoughtful.

Wiesner, Jerome. Special Assistant to the President for Science and Technology (the so-called Science Adviser). An MIT physicist of distinction, experienced in advisory roles, and also in arms control issues. Lacking the terse, one-two-three, analytic style of JFK, Bell, Bundy, McNamara, among others, Wiesner had a more circuitous style that sometimes cost him Kennedy's attention.

Yarmolinsky, Adam. Special Assistant to McNamara. A scholarly lawyer, hard-working, intelligent, prickly on the exterior but warm within, devoted to his boss whom he had not known before he helped recruit him late in 1960. Yarmolinsky was then in turn recruited by McNamara for this job, a new creation.

Zuckert, Eugene. Secretary of the Air Force. Another hard worker, varied experience, faster on his feet than recent predecessors.

British in November 1962

Amery, Julian. Minister of Aviation. Concerned with the industry, production, and trade, not part of the Air Force but an interested bystander, the more so as its recent minister (the PM's son-in-law to boot).

Bligh, Timothy. Principal Private Secretary to the PM. Heroic naval service in World War II followed by a Treasury career; intensely loyal to Macmillan.

Brandon, Henry. Well-known British journalist with exceptional access in both governments, the product of discretion; a long-time specialist in American affairs as Washington correspondent of the London *Sunday Times*.

Brown, George. Shadow Foreign Secretary and Deputy Leader of the Labour Party. An imaginative intelligence and tempestuous personality.

Butler, R. A. ("Rab"). Deputy Prime Minister. Subtle, clever patrician and very senior Tory, whose prewar support of appeasement had damaged his otherwise substantial reputation.

Caccia, Sir Harold. Permanent Under-Secretary of State for Foreign Affairs. The most senior official at the FO, previously Ambassador to Washington

Cary, Michael. Acting Cabinet Secretary. He had had a predominantly Treasury career, but with postings to NATO and to the Air Ministry: conscientious, intelligent, imaginative, son of the novelist Joyce Cary.

de Zulueta, Philip. Private Secretary to the PM (foreign affairs). Keen, quick, yet thoughtful. After six years in the Foreign Service he had been seconded to 10 Downing Street in 1955, survived Eden, and had remained there ever since at the insistence of Macmillan, to whom he, in turn, was devoted

Fraser, Hugh. Secretary of State for Air. A passionate, right-wing, acerbic war hero and supporter of Suez.

Gore, David. So known by his friends. See Ormsby Gore.

Hawthorne, William. Adviser to the Ministry of Defence. Professor of Applied Thermodynamics at Cambridge University and Visiting Professor at MIT, a veritable embodiment of the "special relationship."

Heath, Edward. Lord Privy Seal. The Cabinet minister charged with negotiating British entry into EEC, as it then was; a senior Tory MP and future PM, resolute and single-mindedly pro-European.

Hockaday, Arthur. Private Secretary to Thorneycroft. An Admiralty civil servant since 1949, discreet, conscientious, and in his minister's confidence.

Home, Lord. Secretary of State for Foreign Affairs. This was his latest post in a lifetime of public service as an aristocratic Tory, to be crowned a year hence by brief succession to Macmillan, serving as Sir Alec Douglas-Home (having renounced his peerage for the purpose).

Macmillan, Harold. A one-nation Tory in Parliament from the 1930s, close to Eisenhower since North Africa in the '40s, complex, shrewd, detached and tough behind a bland, Edwardian exterior. Macmillan's private humor and wry outlook on life endeared him to Kennedy, despite their age difference.

Maudling, Reginald. Chancellor of the Exchequer. Clever if somewhat indolent, senior Conservative.

McLeod, Ian. Leader of the House of Commons. Brilliant Tory radical, former Colonial Secretary, regarded by many as a future prime minister (but was to die prematurely).

Mountbatten, Lord. Chief of Defence Staff and Admiral. Had had a distinguished naval career with wartime commands in South Asia and notable service as the last Viceroy of India; doubly related to the Queen; later murdered by the IRA.

Ormsby Gore, Sir David (later Lord Harlech). Ambassador to the United States and a JFK friend. Former Tory MP, intelligent, sensitive, quick on the uptake and well connected: related both to Macmillan's wife and to Kennedy's late lamented brother-in-law, the Marquis of Hartington, killed in World War II.

Sandys, Duncan. Secretary of State for Commonwealth and Colonial Affairs. Popular in the Tory Party, rather on the right.

Scott, Sir Robert. Permanent Under-Secretary, Ministry of Defence. Dry, direct, thoughtful, deeply embedded in the management of his Department, a "mandarin" without airs.

Thorneycroft, Peter. Secretary of State for Defence. A senior Tory MP and former Chancellor of the Exchequer respected—but not advantaged—for having resigned that post on a point of fiscal principle, newly back in Cabinet. Intelligent, analytic, ambitious, a cool customer.

Watkinson, Harold. Thorneycroft's predecessor at Defence. He had been with Macmillan at Camp David in 1960 and had vigorously defended Skybolt to the House of Commons ever since, until dropped in "Macmillan's Purge" the summer of 1962, for no greater offense, apparently, than dullness.

By way of introduction, it remains only to offer a promised document, the memo from JFK formally authorizing my inquiry. This appears on the next page. My report then follows as Chapter 2.

THE WHITE HOUSE
WASHINGTON

March 13, 1963

MEMORANDUM FOR THOSE CONCERNED

Subject: Assignment to Consultant

Professor Richard Neustadt of Columbia University is a member of the
panel of consultants on government structure and operation which I
named in 1961 to assist us from time to time.

In this connection I have asked him now to take a close look at our policy-
making in certain critical fields. By way of subject-matter for detailed review, I have suggested to him aspects of our work on Atlantic Alliance and
related problems since last summer. As a regular consultant he is cleared
for this assignment.

When his study is completed he will make a confidential report for our internal use. I ask that he have full cooperation from all concerned.

/s/ John Kennedy

2

The Report of 1963

REPORT TO THE PRESIDENT

"SKYBOLT AND NASSAU:

American Policy-Making and Anglo-American Relations"

November 15, 1963

(Declassified April 15, 1992)

THE WHITE HOUSE

WASHINGTON

November 15, 1963

Dear Mr. President:

Last March you asked me, in my capacity as a consultant on government operations, "to take a close look at our policy-making in certain critical fields," using as case material "aspects of our work on Atlantic Alliance and related problems." In April we agreed that I would focus on events surrounding SKYBOLT cancellation and the Nassau Conference, with reference both to what occurred inside our government and to relations with the British Government.

My report on these events is attached. I have chosen to present them as a story, rather than to treat them as a source of observations. The story is of more use, I believe, than an extended commentary.

In the course of this study I have interviewed and read the files of virtually all participants in these events at every level of our government. Everyone has been cooperative beyond the call of duty. I acknowledge this with gratitude. I have also interviewed a number of participants and key observers in the British Government, and have seen selected files of the Prime Minister's Private Office. British cooperation is a tribute to you, not to me, but I am no less grateful for that! Regarding the French who enter this study as "noises off stage," I have not, for obvious reasons, tried interviewing in the Elysée. Along with British and American official sources I have had access to a manuscript, based on Paris interviews, prepared by Robert Klieman for the Council on Foreign Relations. His study will be published by the Council in December.

For the sake of perspective I have pursued strands of policy back to the Spring of 1961 or even earlier, and forward through the course of MLF this year. These earlier and later matters are not touched in the attached report, unless they bear directly on "Skybolt" and "Nassau." But as a generalization I am now able to say that the administrative behavior and policy perspectives here described are not uncharacteristic.

Respectfully,

Richard E. Neustadt
Consultant

The President
The White House

SKYBOLT AND NASSAU

Contents

I. Introduction

On December 11, 1962 in London, Secretary of Defense Robert McNamara met Peter Thorneycroft, the British Defence Minister, to continue a discussion they had started on the telephone, November 9. Their subject was a substitute for SKYBOLT, the planned American air-to-surface missile on which London had relied to prolong life for its manned-bomber nuclear deterrent, but which Washington now wanted to abandon. In the course of their meeting each man got a severe shock. Each discovered that the other did not say and evidently had not done what was expected from him on the basis of that phone call. What were their expectations, and how formed? Why did they let a month go by before they checked them out? Answers to these questions are the heart of the Skybolt story.

On December 18, 1962, in Nassau, the Bahamas, President Kennedy met Prime Minister Macmillan; they picked up where their Ministers left off. They greeted one another just two days after Macmillan had concluded an unpleasant interview at Rambouillet with Charles de Gaulle of France. At this juncture the President and the Prime Minister shared high-priority objectives: British entry into EEC, a British role in "Europe," transatlantic "partnership." They also shared a pressing problem: French hostility. But the two men could not focus on that problem. The Prime Minister could not acquaint the President with what they had to face in light of Rambouillet. Instead he had to concentrate on squeezing out of Kennedy POLARIS as a substitute for SKYBOLT. And Kennedy could not persuade Macmillan to defer decision on that substitute, never mind its likely look to Europe. Instead he had to concentrate on improvising what he wanted from Macmillan in return. Why did the one man feel impelled to put the squeeze upon the other? Why did the other have to *improvise* his *quid pro quo*? Why were they both unable to keep their minds on de Gaulle? Answers to these questions are the heart of the Nassau story.

"Nassau" resolved "Skybolt." From American officials the terms of resolution won a mixed reception. Just before the Nassau Conference closed, one senior member of the American delegation phoned a State Department colleague to inquire, "How does it look up there?" The answer: "A disaster." Another senior member, relaxing on the flight back to the States, told an associate: "If 'Skybolt' hadn't happened it should have been invented to get us set on this new track of viable policy." Three weeks later, de Gaulle's January press conference stilled claims of "viability," and sharpened allegations of "disaster."

In retrospect, both these descriptions miss the mark. To be sure, that "new track" has yet to reach a destination. As this is written, MLF is not in sight; IANF has not left the station; negotiation with the French has still to start. On the other hand, de Gaulle's hostility toward British membership in EEC and his insistence on a national deterrent for himself were not "caused" by the Nassau Conference and would not have disappeared had there been no such conference. December's public spectacle of Anglo-Saxon Attitudes helped his choice of means, January's "thunderbolt." I know of nothing to suggest that Nassau changed his aims. But many things suggest that without Nassau's terms, London would have been estranged from Washington at least for the short run, perhaps for a long time. In this sense certainly, the Conference was no "disaster." In this sense also, "Nassau" almost surely had to follow upon "Skybolt."

As an issue in Anglo-American relations, "Skybolt" has been charged to many causes: to "arbitrary" budgeting, to lack of consultation with the State Department, to lack of warning for the British, to "usurpation" by Defense of State's negotiating role. These attributions are all wide of the mark. The budget decision was *not* arbitrary, State *was* consulted, the British *were* warned, Defense did *not* usurp.

"Skybolt" as an issue between Washington and London was caused by none of these but by successive failures on the part of busy persons to perceive and make allowance for the needs and wants of others: failures among "Chiefs" to share their reasoning with "Indians"; failures among Indians to sense—or heed—the reservations of their Chiefs; failures among Americans to comprehend restraints upon contingency-planning in London; failures among Englishmen to comprehend imperatives of budgeting in Washington; failures on all sides to consider how A's conduct might tie B's tongue.

Some of these were sheer "communication" failures. By accident, or by design, word did not pass. But more important were the failures to seek and obtain *feed-back*. A word was passed but speakers did not pause to check what auditors had on their minds before and after listening. And auditors heard mostly what their minds were set to hear, in light of their own hopes and fears, their stakes, their risks, regardless of the speaker's. When Chiefs worked without Indians deliberately, they often failed to arrange feed-back for *themselves*. When Chiefs relied on Indians, their aides quite often failed to do it for them.

Beneath these proximate causes lies a basic failure reaching back to 1960, to the Eisenhower regime: a failure to assure that Britain's defense posture and Anglo-American cooperation rested on a rationale which could be justified in technical and military terms, *since these were the ostensible terms*, as well as in implicit terms of diplomatic and domestic politics.

Such were the causes of "Skybolt" as an issue during 1962. To show the causes is to tell the story.

II. Budgetary Prelude

Early in November 1962, the Secretary of Defense put to the President and to the Secretary of State the likelihood that we would terminate our SKYBOLT program. As an active issue in Washington and London, the Skybolt story then began. But what occurred thereafter is best understood by light of answers to some prior questions: What brought the Defense Secretary to the White House then? What were his expectations then? What were the President's, and State's, and London's? With what stakes and perspectives did the actors in this story start? For answers one goes back two months in time to an early, quiet stage of budget season at the Pentagon.

The reasons for the quiet are a factor in the story.

On August 24, 1962, the Controller of the Pentagon and the Director

of Defense Research and Engineering, Charles Hitch and Harold
Brown, met Secretary McNamara to discuss in confidence their latest
studies of the SKYBOLT program. These studies had been made at his request. The weapon, at this juncture, was still under development after
two years of effort, and at least another two years would be needed to
reach full production. The Brown and Hitch reports, though separately
prepared, came to the same conclusion:

> The . . . SKYBOLT force, as part . . . of a . . . B-52 force, is inferior to
> the force which could be bought for a somewhat smaller amount of
> money by filling out the B-52 squadrons with HOUND DOG missiles
> and buying a certain number of additional MINUTEMEN. . . . The SKY-
> BOLTS themselves are to be used either for defense suppression (which
> is the principal purpose of the HOUND DOG missiles) or against pri-
> mary targets (which can also be attacked by MINUTEMAN).

A good deal more than money was involved in this conclusion.
HOUND DOG, like SKYBOLT, was an air-to-surface weapon, although
it lacked SKYBOLT's range. MINUTEMAN was a solid-fueled, surface-to-
surface weapon with intercontinental range:

> . . . HOUND DOG has completed its development, and MINUTEMAN will
> do so by the end of this year, whereas SKYBOLT will take another two
> years . . . the difference in schedule is likely to be reflected, as well, in
> a lower reliability for SKYBOLT. . . . the risk that SKYBOLT will fail to
> work at all is very low; the risk that it will not be a highly reliable . . .
> system until the late 1960's is quite large.

By the late 1960's defense suppression for manned bombers would be
rendered moot if bombers then were phasing out of our strategic forces.
Meanwhile, we had HOUND DOG. As for primary attack, where reliability mattered less, MINUTEMAN was now at hand; SKYBOLT was not.

This line of argument was not new to the three men meeting in the
Secretary's office. In the last year of the Eisenhower Administration
when SKYBOLT got its start, Brown had chaired a PSAC panel which reported negatively on the weapon and on its guidance system, key to
reliability. In the first year of the Kennedy Administration, Hitch had
viewed with sympathy efforts by Presidential aides—Carl Kaysen,
Jerome Wiesner and the Budget Director, David Bell—to persuade
McNamara that the weapon should be dropped. That effort, in Bell's

phrase, had been a "near-miss" during budget season 1961. Now, ten
months later, Hitch was reviving it.

As for McNamara himself, SKYBOLT had been among the problem-
items on which he and Bell were briefed by Budget aides before the
Kennedy Inaugural. SKYBOLT then was virtually stalled for lack of development funds which McNamara's predecessor, Thomas Gates, had chosen to withhold. (Gates had been both irritated at the Air Force and in
doubt about the program.) One of McNamara's early actions was to re-
store funds for full development. He in his turn, after Gates, had then
been treated both to slippages in schedule and to increases in cost. During the fall of 1961, McNamara had resisted urgings from the Presidential staff to drop the program. Instead, he had devised a sort of treaty
with the Air Force, setting a fixed ceiling for total development costs.
By the spring of 1962 it had become clear that the "treaty" would be
breached. The Air Force now asked urgently that he release production
funds with which—in effect if not form—to carry on development.
This request was on his desk along with the reports of Brown and
Hitch.

The Air Force asked for funds with confidence. McNamara had just
won a year-long battle with the Service and its Congressional supporters
on the future of the RS-70. His victory spelled doom, in time, for the
manned bomber. But his victory also left scars, among other places on
Capitol Hill. In Air Force circles it was thought unlikely that he would
tempt fate by striking at another cherished program while the echoes of
the RS-70 dispute could still be heard.

Moreover, the Air Force knew—as McNamara, Hitch, and Brown did
also—that the SKYBOLT program had been undertaken to meet British
purposes as well as ours, and that the British Government was totally
dependent on the program to maintain its current version of a nuclear
deterrent after the mid-1960's. Manned aircraft—the V-bombers—
were the only British strike-forces at hand or in development. Soviet
defense measures progressively decreased their capability. SKYBOLT was
expected to renew it and maintain it for at least five years. British claims
to status as a nuclear power, in possession of an independent nuclear deterrent, were thus mortgaged to SKYBOLT, *not* as a weapon of defense
suppression but as *the* means of mounting an attack.

Besides, the British Government had more at stake than nuclear status. Military power was the surface of the issue; beneath lay Tory power.
The Labour opposition had decried the whole deterrent posture; Labour

spokesmen had poured scorn on SKYBOLT as a weapon; right-wing Tory back-benchers had criticized dependence on Americans. Macmillan, meanwhile, had defended everything and his Defence Minister's supporting case had often been extravagant. Macmillan's reputation, frontbench credibility and Tory solidarity were linked with the success of SKYBOLT.

An Air Force general told a Budget Bureau aide in 1962: "They can't cancel SKYBOLT on us. The British are in with us. They won't do that to them." In the event his confidence was misplaced, but the prior history of SKYBOLT gave him ample grounds for it. Indeed, the two Air Forces, ours and theirs, had used each other's leverage continuously and effectively from SKYBOLT's first beginnings. Harold Watkinson, the then Defence Minister, recalls that late in 1959 when the British were deciding to abandon BLUE STREAK (their surface-to-surface missile) because of mounting costs combined with RAF distaste for "sitting in silos," there came a "bolt out of the blue": reports of American enthusiasm for SKYBOLT. John Rubel, then a technical assistant to the Secretary of Defense, recalls that Gates was pressed to proceed with SKYBOLT partly by reports "that this was what the British wanted."

Considerable testimony, some of it from Watkinson, suggests that at Camp David in March 1960, when we agreed to British purchases of SKYBOLT, Gates and Watkinson alike would have been pleased had the other shown strong preference for a British share, instead, in POLARIS. If so, the SKYBOLT program started as it was to end, with transatlantic reticence from Minister to Minister occasioned by the intimacy of their Air Forces.

For Hitch and Brown on August 24, awaiting word from McNamara, British stakes in SKYBOLT did not seem the barrier to cancellation which our Air Force may have thought them. The Camp David agreement, on its face, had done no more than pledge that the Americans would make SKYBOLT available to Britain if successfully developed, with consultation specified should we give up the effort. Consultation there would have to be, and some agreed alternative devised. No doubt the British would not find this easy and would not be pleased. But from the vantage point of the Defense Controller, and his colleague the Director of Research, British displeasure was dwarfed by the prospect of Congressional displeasure.

The Air Force—and the Douglas Corporation as prime contractor—were anything but friendless on the Hill. They and their friends shared common views, and also shared the scars of McNamara's war on RS-70.

Renewed combat was risky. Congressional pressure might suffice to force reversal of a SKYBOLT cancellation, or at least to penalize Defense in other ways.

How could the risk be minimized? Hitch had a formula: SKYBOLT should vanish in the course of budget season, disappearing from the January Budget with the current program cancelled as the budget went to Congress. Then proponents of the program would face a *fait accompli*. They, not Defense, would have to change the *status quo*. And they would have to make their case for change against the backdrop of a massive budget deficit combined with calls for tax cuts. In August 1962 that backdrop seemed assured.

On this logic, the time to cancel SKYBOLT was not August but December. Hitch conveyed the point to McNamara.

On August 24 the Secretary needed no prompting. Somewhat to the surprise of his two aides, but to their pleasure, he indicated that he saw the substance and the tactics much as they did. They left his office clear in their minds on several scores: McNamara was prepared to deal with SKYBOLT on the technical and budgetary merits of the case and then to cope with consequences, British and Congressional. He was prepared to recommend a cancellation when the time came; the time was not yet. He also would absorb the new requirement for MINUTEMAN without a net addition to the missiles now on order; this would magnify the savings gained from cancellation.

Meanwhile, McNamara would not telegraph his punches, nor should they. He would release production funds (he did so in September), but only month-by-month. The Air Force thus would know SKYBOLT was under scrutiny, but "premature" reactions would be stifled by the money.

Hitch and Brown returned to their offices and kept their mouths shut. Each told his deputy, Alain Enthoven and John Rubel, that the outlook was for cancellation later, silence now. Apparently no more was said by any of the four to anybody for at least a month, and precious little until late October. Secrecy has rarely been as well maintained as by these men—and McNamara.

III. October Interlude

In mid-September 1962, Peter Thorneycroft paid his first visit to Washington since taking office as Defence Minister, July 13, when Watkinson, one among seven, left precipitously in "Macmillan's Purge," the move

toward a "new look" for the Tories. Thorneycroft had been a senior
Minister before as Chancellor of the Exchequer, a post he had resigned
early in 1959 on a "matter of principle." This evoked abstract admira-
tion but no tangible support from his back-benchers and the press.
In 1960 he had joined the Government again as Minister of Aviation
(where, incidentally, he had first encountered SKYBOLT). His new port-
folio restored him to a senior place, less senior than before but moving
in the right direction.

Washington gave Thorneycroft a warm reception. The President
scooped him up and took him off on tour of missile test-sites and research facilities. McNamara took him out to SAC. In the process there
was a good deal of conversation, some of it on SKYBOLT.

McNamara, understandably, did not pursue that subject very far:
Thorneycroft-to-RAF-to-USAF was too obvious a channel of communication. The Secretary told the Minister that he was now releasing some
production funds; he also indicated that he was disturbed by rising costs
and lagging schedules in development. The first item of information evidently meant more to Thorneycroft than the second. In a program of
development he thought it natural that cost and time should exceed estimates. *His* concern was with what followed after, and the release of
production funds had a good sound. He did take care, however, to expound to McNamara, and briefly to the President, the British need for
SKYBOLT and the British understanding that the essence of Camp David
was our help for their deterrent. This told his auditors nothing they had
not heard before, but perhaps conveyed a nuance which they missed.

Regarding McNamara's private plans for SKYBOLT, Thorneycroft de-
parted no wiser than he came. His Embassy in Washington and Ministry in London were no wiser than he. Their own links to the program
were extensive: technical staffs in Washington and California kept them
close to our Air Force and to the Douglas Corporation; our attachés
and Corporation representatives in London returned the compliment.
But as information sources these had two deficiencies: they did not rep-
resent the third floor of the Pentagon, and they had a vested interest in
"selling" the program.

Only Solly Zuckerman, the Ministry's chief scientist, was close to
higher sources: Brown's office at Defense, Wiesner's at the White House.
But Zuckerman, like his American friends, had never been a SKYBOLT
partisan—far from it. He had never made a secret of his disdain for its
guidance system. In the Ministries of Air and Aviation he was tagged as

something of a "traitor." His warnings roused more anger than attention. Besides, in September he heard nothing from Brown's office and
Wiesner's office heard nothing from Brown.

London did not know, but neither did official Washington. Not until
late September was Paul Nitze's Office of International Security Affairs
clued in on what impended; and Nitze was McNamara's own man, an
Assistant Secretary of Defense. Not until then was Wiesner's office able
to extract a solid hint; and Wiesner had the services of Spurgeon Keeny,
perhaps the best intelligence-operative in the Executive Office Building.
Keeny passed a word to friends in State; for reasons I will mention in
due course his friends remained unruffled. By then the Budget Bureau
staff had learned enough, through Keeny among others, to seek the
word directly. They got it, under pledge of secrecy, from McNamara's
Deputy, Roswell Gilpatric. But this did not occur until October 15.

The Cuban crisis then took center-stage.

At the height of the crisis, October 26, Budget Director Bell sent a
memorandum to McGeorge Bundy at the White House. This had been
drafted by Bell's Military Division a week after Gilpatric's revelation.
The draft was first intended as a memorandum for the President; in the
circumstances Bell had told his staff to change the addressee. Bell's
memorandum gave it as his understanding ". . . that the current reviews
in Defense in connection with the 1964 budget will lead to a firm recommendation by the Secretary that development of the SKYBOLT missile
be cancelled." Bell indicated that the Budget Bureau had no quarrel
with this (indeed he personally had urged it on the Secretary in July),
but noted that it raised an issue in the foreign field which someone else
should check and button up:

> . . . cancellation is likely to create internal political problems for the
> British . . . our actions up to now, while not actually committing us,
> have clearly implied an intention to proceed. . . . It would seem im-
> portant that suitable arrangements be made for advance
> notification . . . and consultation prior to the time that a decision be-
> comes known publicly or through Air Force channels. . . .

Bundy, embroiled with Cuba, scarcely saw this memorandum but
his deputy, Carl Kaysen, who was serving momentarily as "Bundy-for-
everything-else," put it on his own work list. Kaysen was no stranger to
the SKYBOLT issue, or to Defense and State. On October 31 he talked by

phone with Nitze at Defense and then called William Tyler, the Assistant Secretary of State for European Affairs. Kaysen gave Tyler the essence of the story, confidentially, and asked him for a quick appraisal of the British problem and of London's probable reaction. Tyler passed the task to BNA, the British desk in the Department. A response from the desk officers reached him two days later. On November 2 he sent their memorandum to the White House.

This was a moment of glory for the men in BNA, traditionally the least consulted country-desk at State since high officials from the President down are bound to be "desk officers" on Britain. Having suddenly acquired an unlooked-for opportunity, these men made all they could of it:

> Cancellation of SKYBOLT would put in jeopardy not only Bomber Command but a vital element of British defense philosophy . . . the independent nuclear deterrent.
>
> Two of the Conservative Party's talking points are that they have special and superior qualifications, as compared with Labour, for dealing with 1) defense and 2) the Americans. . . . Cancellation . . . could be an unmitigated political blow to the Conservatives. . . . Whatever our own feelings about the efficacy of [their] deterrent, the British could hardly regard our cancelling SKYBOLT as a friendly gesture. . . .
>
> . . . [They] would certainly feel let down—hard. . . . We still rely heavily on British real estate all over the world from Christmas Island to Holy Loch. We should carefully consider the consequences of an estrangement.
>
> . . . Assuming that a decision has already been made . . . urgent consideration must be given to the manner and timing of informing the British. . . . [Macmillan] should have as much time as possible to prepare the ground before an announcement is made. . . .

Two assumptions ran through the entire memorandum: an "independent deterrent" was inseparable from SKYBOLT, and Macmillan could put time to use if he were given some. As events would show, these two assumptions hid the heart of the British problem. But the authors of this memorandum were only the first of our officials to be led astray by their assumptions. Soon they would have a lot of company.

To a degree, the European Bureau now worked in the dark. Witness those assumptions. The men in BNA had not been there when the SKYBOLT Agreement was made. Nor, for that matter, had Tyler. None of

them were informed at first-hand about the origins of what they now
described. The State Department officers who seem to have known most
about events in 1960 had been transferred overseas a mere three months
before: Foy Kohler, Tyler's predecessor, and one of his assistants, Russell Fessenden. In November 1962, Rubel of Defense was the one senior
official on the scene with roughly the same role regarding SKYBOLT as
in 1960.

While this memorandum was in preparation at our State Department, Rubel arrived in London for technical talks on other subjects. On
November 3, Thorneycroft invited him into a private session and confronted him with rumors that SKYBOLT was in deep trouble. Rubel knew
of recent press reports to that effect, but Thorneycroft's concern was
with more substantial stuff. Whitehall, he said, was full of talk. So it
was: as Thorneycroft did not tell Rubel, British diplomatic staff—not
the technicians—at their Embassy had got onto the story some days
earlier through hints from friends in McNamara's entourage. Rubel,
bound by secrecy, could say no more than that normal reviews were
now in progress. His response did not suffice for Thorneycroft.

On November 5, Thorneycroft cabled McNamara. The cable conveyed a message, delicately done. The Minister began by noting that
"the British press report what they describe as the 'first production order for Skybolt'. . . . you will not be surprised when I say this is welcome news indeed." There followed a few cheery generalities and then
a final sentence: "We look forward to . . . success with the Skybolt pro-
gramme, which is, as you know, a central feature both of our defense
policy and of our collaboration with you."

This piece of English understatement reached the Pentagon the day
that McNamara sent to the Joint Chiefs of Staff, for their advice, his
draft budget proposals on strategic retaliatory forces. SKYBOLT was
missing from the column for the coming year. There could be no American "decision" until the Chiefs responded and the *President* decided.
But with McNamara's own position stated, matters had proceeded very
far. The Chiefs were to be heard from by November 20; the President's
review would follow promptly. Decision was in sight within the month.

Thorneycroft's last sentence made it plain that he would have to be
enlightened, and at once. Nitze's office drafted a reply by cable; McNamara thought this insufficient, in terms both of British needs and of his
own intention. Instead he asked to see the President and telephoned
Dean Rusk, the Secretary of State. On November 7, four days after
Rubel had seen Thorneycroft and five days after Kaysen had got Tyler's

memorandum, McNamara and Nitze, joined by Rusk and Bundy, met to discuss SKYBOLT in the presence of the President.

With preliminaries over, *and no harm done yet*, the story now begins.

IV. Washington Warns London

November 7 was the eleventh day after the climactic Sunday of the Cuba crisis. The five men meeting at the White House had that Sunday still in mind; the crisis had passed, or been suspended anyway, but Soviet missiles were barely off the island, and I1-28's [bombers] remained to be pried off in the next weeks. Moreover, for those five men "Cuba" had been an extraordinary test, *the* problem of their lives, rendering their other problems minor by comparison. They had lived through the experience together, had got over the hump together. Now in the aftermath they were relieved, and confident, and close. They also were at work together on a new concern: Chinese troops were marching against India.

In this context they met to deal with Thorneycroft's problem. McNamara sketched the situation. He already had given Rusk the gist of it, as Tyler had done also, and Bundy knew of it from Kaysen. The President had heard enough from his own aides the year before and had been thinking hard enough about his budget deficit to find the proposition that he cancel SKYBOLT no surprise, and quite acceptable. McNamara's budgeting would save $2.5 billion over several fiscal years, a fifth of it in the next year alone. McNamara's tactics should assure the saving, while a year's delay could jeopardize the whole: with half a billion more invested, Air Force friends in Congress would be hard to stop; witness the RS-70. Foreign policy considerations did not justify foregoing all that money. Rusk agreed.

The issue then was how to compensate the British. McNamara and Rusk both told the President, as each recalls, that London would be left with quite a problem: "It may be so serious as to make the Government fall." No one wanted that. They also felt, and stated, that Camp David and our conduct since left us committed morally to join in some replacement for the SKYBOLT Agreement, if London so desired as a way to meet the problem. There was some mention of POLARIS as a possibility, but specifics were not much discussed. The British would need time to think through their desires, programmatic and political. We ought to warn them now and then consult with them once we were done with our decision-making, three weeks hence.

With all of this the President agreed and turned to the mechanics: how to tell the British so they could collect their thoughts without suggesting to our Air Force that "decision" had preceded word from the Joint Chiefs. Not remarkably, the President's solution was to call upon his friend the British Ambassador, Sir David Ormsby Gore. McNamara volunteered to do that. He also volunteered to talk by phone with Thorneycroft. "I'll take care of it," he offered. The others said, "That's fine." The five then turned to other subjects.

These men never did assume what State's desk officers had done, that Britain's status as possessor of an "independent deterrent" was synonymous with the SKYBOLT Agreement. On the contrary, they took it for granted that if London chose to keep the status—as seemed likely—something else could substitute for the Agreement. That would be negotiable when we had reached the stage of consultation. In the meantime it was up to London to decide what London wanted: the problem was theirs, not ours. The English, after all, were "clever chaps"; with time they'd work it out. And time was what we now proposed to give.

In actuality, from where Macmillan stood, and Thorneycroft, if time was all we offered it was little use to them. But the men at the White House did not know that. In this respect they saw no more than BNA had done. What State had not picked up they were in no position to suck out of their own thumbs. Macmillan's problem had its roots in a decision taken with Dwight Eisenhower at Camp David; none of them had been there. And it did not occur to Bundy or the President to use their private telephone. McNamara would "take care of it."

The Secretary of Defense was quick to carry out his mandate. The next day, November 8, he saw the British Ambassador and told him all he could: successive increases in cost were causing us to reconsider SKY-BOLT's worth; cancellation (he implied) was now a likely prospect; he awaited recommendations from the Chiefs and no decision would be made for "three or four weeks," but London ought to know that we were reconsidering. Gore responded strongly, with an undertone of passion: if SKYBOLT were cancelled his Government faced an "immense" political problem, a "political disaster" which could not be warded off by any substitute.

Gore returned to Massachusetts Avenue in shock. What he had heard confirmed, outran the recent rumors. A compatriot who saw him later in the day recalls that he "was like a man who'd learned the Bomb was going to drop, the end of civilization, and he doubted he could stop it." Whatever his feelings, he lost no time in sending off a full account of his exchange with McNamara. Gore's dispatch did not say that SKYBOLT necessarily was gone for good; no one had told him so and privately he thought the issue still negotiable; he emphasized, however, that it was in "serious jeopardy." His theme was "peril"; he pursued it for two pages.

This Embassy dispatch was passed to Thorneycroft before a phone call came from McNamara. By prearrangement, the latter waited a day. He called November 9. He gave the Minister the substance of what he had said to the Ambassador. Then, as he noted at the time:

> I added that in the event it appeared desirable for the U.S. to cancel the SKYBOLT program, I believed there would be several alternatives that should be considered by the British. . . . Further, I stated that prior to any U.S. decision to cancel I would be quite willing to come to London to discuss the matter with Peter. I estimated that the decision would not be made here before approximately December 10. London consultations would probably not be advisable before November 23rd.

December 10 was actually *not* the date when McNamara foresaw an American decision. November 23 was when he hoped for final clearance from the President, which is why he used it as he did in this conversation. December 10 was, rather, what he subsequently put to Nitze as the "probable leak-date" of the decision, a week after normal budgetary practice would have got the final word to the Joint Chiefs. The seventeen-day difference in his dating of "decision" was not meant to confuse London but merely to give McNamara added leeway. He did not intend confusion; in the event he caused some.

Thorneycroft's response was brief and to the point. Few words were wasted on complaint, none on recrimination. His hearer caught the tone and later commented to Nitze, "He was less excited than I'd expected, judging from David Gore." McNamara noted at the time that Thorneycroft:

> . . . suggested that before we met in London it would be useful for him to have a memorandum outlining our views. Further, he stated his appreciation of the advance notice . . . of our reconsideration . . . and he stated he would immediately arrange for his department to consider how the V-bomber force might be operated without Skybolt and what the U.S. and British Governments should state to the public in the event the program is cancelled. Thorneycroft implied his Gov-

ernment would wish to consider a sub-launched missile if it appeared
the V-bomber force would be made obsolete by the loss of SKYBOLT.

This squares with Thorneycroft's own recollection, save in one particular: "I did more than intimate; I used the *word* 'POLARIS.' I said I
thought we'd have to start from there. I assumed he'd get the message."

At about the time these men talked on the telephone, Zuckerman was
hearing on another phone of SKYBOLT's definite demise. His informant
was Will Hawthorne, Professor of Engineering in Cambridge University
and a Ministry consultant, who currently combined a visiting year at
MIT with frequent trips to Washington. Hawthorne indicated he had
learned enough from friends to know that McNamara's words covered a
definite intention: SKYBOLT *would* be cancelled. (Bundy was his source,
although he did not say so.) Zuckerman felt no surprise; Rubel had
"opened his mind" to him a week before, as well as in months past. He
had kept Rubel's confidence; this was another matter. Hawthorne's
word was duly passed to Thorneycroft. As Zuckerman recalls, it seemed
to make no impact.

Hawthorne had attempted to do more than sharpen McNamara's
warning. He had sought to caution his American friends. On November 7, following a conversation the preceding evening, he saw Bundy
and endeavored to convey the situation as he sensed it: if we dropped
SKYBOLT the heart of *their* problem became *our* substitute. Hawthorne
spent no time on a defense of SKYBOLT. Unlike Gore, he shared with
Wiesner, Brown, and Zuckerman a scientist's dubiety about its guid-
ance-system. But granting we should junk it, what were we prepared to
do, instead, for them? Bundy grew a bit impatient. He recalls asking
"what do you need, what do you want?" The burden of his comment
was "figure it out and tell us." If the answer were POLARIS, he suggested
they could have it. But the decision was theirs, not ours; it was their
problem. Hawthorne recalls doubting "they" would see it so; hence his
London phone call, two days later. Thereafter, he felt *he* could do no
more, lest he be catalogued as anti-RAF. Bundy, meanwhile, turned to
other things. The British chaps and McNamara had this one in hand.

The Secretary of Defense, for his part, saw another transatlantic duty
which it seemed to him he should perform. He asked Nitze's office to
prepare a cable for the American Ambassador in London, David Bruce.
This went to Bruce, "Eyes Only," on November 12, "to bring you up to
date." It indicated SKYBOLT's state and summarized what had been said
to Gore and Thorneycroft, including McNamara's offer to come over af-

ter November 23, "for a discussion of alternatives open to the British."
Bruce was told he would be kept advised.

On the Secretary's instruction a copy of this cable was sent to his colleague, the Secretary of State. Rusk did not share it with the State Department, nor did McNamara: the original reached Bruce through military channels.

McNamara, meanwhile, had put Nitze's staff to work on something
else: a look into alternatives which British staffs could be expected to
consider. If he were going over there he wanted to be sure that while
the British did their homework we did ours; he meant to be at least as
well prepared as they to pass on what was sensible for them and sound
for us. After he had finished talking to their Minister November 9, he
told Nitze to get studies started on alternatives and indicated those he
thought most promising: first, HOUND DOG or a variant to substitute
for SKYBOLT, if British bombers could adapt to carry it; second, a British take-over of SKYBOLT development, with some financial aid from
us; and third, a substitution of POLARIS. Whether or not he heard that
word, the thing was in his mind as worth exploring.

Nitze at once assembled a mixed group from his office and Brown's.
They discussed these alternatives and added a fourth: British participation in a mixed-manned, multilateral, MRBM force, a "Smith-Lee"
force, of which more later. Nitze then parcelled out assignments. One of
his deputies, Harry Rowen, received several of these, with special reference to political aspects, and ended as the man who pulled the whole
together. Rowen's report went to McNamara two weeks later, on November 23.

The Secretary was not at the Pentagon, November 23. He was in
Hyannis Port, meeting with the President, Bell, Bundy, Wiesner, among
others, on his budget proposals for strategic retaliatory forces. Kaysen,
incidentally, as the White House aide who regularly followed defense
budgeting, would ordinarily have been there but was not. On
November 12 he had emplaned for India with the Harriman mission,
disappearing from the scene—and from this story.

The Joint Chiefs had now been heard from. Comments had arrived
November 20, as expected. Regarding SKYBOLT, the three Service Chiefs,
predictably, had joined to urge continuation of the program; so they had
done each year since 1960. Their Chairman, General Maxwell Taylor,
had demurred. The readiness of other missiles seemed to him sufficient
reason not to tie up funds in this one. On this issue he had filed a separate statement endorsing cancellation. As he recalls:

This was a lot easier for me than for my Army and Navy colleagues. I had only joined them in October, no commitments. They had backed the Air Force Chief before, and had sat with him since. There's a certain honor about these things; I was out of it.

The Hyannis Port meeting did not dwell for long on SKYBOLT. McNamara would have pressed his case had all the Chiefs opposed him; with the Chairman's support there was little need for argument. Since British aspects had been covered on November 7, he did not devote much time to it, nor did the President. Bell, of course, had nothing to dispute. Wiesner, who had been alerted by his English friends, attempted to expound the British problem; Bundy, sensitive to moods and mindful also of the prior meeting, cut him short. Presidential action on the issue was recorded as approving cancellation, "subject to consultation with the British on alternatives."

The Secretary of Defense had a decision; now he had to consult.

V. State Instructs Defense

When Rowen and his associates in ISA, the Nitze office, McNamara's "junior State Department," began studying alternatives for SKYBOLT on November 9, they knew that "senior State," across the river, had pronounced upon the subject rather recently. On September 8, a few days before Thorneycroft reached Washington, Rusk had sent a "Dear Bob" letter to his colleague at Defense:

> You will recall the April 21, 1961 NSC Policy Directive, which states that "over the long run it would be desirable if the British decided to phase out of the nuclear deterrent business." It also states that the US should not prolong the life of the British deterrent, except . . . [for] SKYBOLT if this is warranted for US purposes alone.
>
> The present situation in Europe underscores . . . this policy. After the UK-EEC negotiations, the special US-UK relationship may have to be closely re-examined . . . it is of the utmost importance to avoid any actions to expand the relationship. Such actions could seriously prejudice . . . sound multilateral arrangements. . . .
>
> . . . The British probably feel that the V-bomber force . . . is a wasting asset. . . . They have shown past interest in . . . polaris submarines. They may be considering whether to try . . . to continue a UK national force into the missile era—probably combined with a French national force under some type of "joint" arrangement. . . . Such an arrange-

ment would . . . vastly complicate our efforts to hold pressures for a German national program in check. . . .

I hope therefore that both our staffs can hold to existing policies in discussions with Defense Minister Thorneycroft. . . .

This came two weeks after McNamara set his sights on SKYBOLT; Rusk's letter-writers knew nothing of that.

The signature was Rusk's; the tone was not. McNamara had not paid the letter much attention. He could not see, September 8, why he deserved a lecture, and anyway from private talks he knew Rusk valued the relationship with Britain, at least while nothing better was assured, and doubted "multilateral arrangements." So did he.

Nitze, one step down, had been annoyed. He too disliked the lecture; he was not enamored of its premises. Nitze held a very different view of what was "good" and "bad" in European prospects. He was an advocate of updating the "special relationship" to guard against a British slide toward neutralism. He also advocated upgrading relationships with others, notably the French, to parallel the London connection. His image was not "multilateral arrangements" but bilateral arrangements radiating from our "hub" like "spokes in a wheel." Rusk's letter reflected quite another purpose, which Nitze had opposed before and would again. But now he judged that Rusk was not the source and let it go at that.

Lower down the ladder in the Pentagon, however, distinctions between Rusk and State were blurred by the man's signature. Some of Nitze's uniformed subordinates, especially those closest to the British situation, felt inhibited thereafter; SKYBOLT cancellation on the one hand, and withholding of POLARIS on the other, seemed beyond the realm of argument for them: senior State had spoken.

Rowen, for his part, had no such inhibitions; he was a civilian, out of RAND to boot. But he knew and had some sympathy for the strong thrust of purpose which the letter of September 8 reflected. He knew the personalities and saw the issues and had read the record. That letter now was in the record, signature included. In examining alternatives, as he was now to do, Rowen thought it well to consult State.

The day Rowen began to look into alternatives, November 9, Tyler at the State Department sent the Secretary of State a memorandum covering the one that he had given Kaysen a week earlier. The week had been spent on clearances. In the clearance-process many offices discovered part of what the Secretary already knew. Reactions varied: the British desk still fretted for the British. Elsewhere in the European Bureau there was indignation at the thought that budgeteers were dominating policy "again." Feeling ran particularly high among the aides to Robert Schaetzel, Tyler's deputy for Regional Affairs. Schaetzel's office was intent on British efforts to join EEC. If SKYBOLT vanished, might the Tories fall? Who then would "take England into Europe"? Hardly Labour. But if we helped the Tories with a substitute for SKYBOLT, what would Europe think about their will to become Europeans? While EEC negotiations lasted, so should SKYBOLT. Any other course would rock the boat.

For a time the cry became: "reverse the budgeteers." Tyler bore with this but gave it no support. A brief talk with the Secretary had informed his sensitive ear that Rusk was not disposed to quarrel with McNamara's budgeting. Tyler recalls asking: "Is there anything I should do?" The Secretary responded, "No; I'm in touch with McNamara and the President."

Schaetzel and his aides were left to contemplate the silver lining: imminent demise of Britain's independent deterrent. The letter of September 8, first drafted as an "action program," had originated in their shop. It had invoked what they assumed to be Administration policy: that a United Europe, linked in transatlantic partnership, should rise on the foundation of an enlarged EEC. Britain's nuclear deterrent was divisive. It already had fueled French ambitions for a national capability; there was hope of a Gaullist defeat in Assembly elections, but even so their national deterrent might be hard to stop. As France proceeded, comparable ambitions someday would become the coin of politics in Bonn. At worst this might spark German adventurism, Soviet preventive action, perhaps both. At least it would impair the growth of European sentiment and institutions, on which we had counted since the 1940's to bind resurgent Germany into the West.

No one had conceived, September 8, that SKYBOLT as an issue would arise so fast. But since it had, perhaps it could be turned to good account: reaffirmation that beyond the V-bombers the British would have no more "independence" than the Germans.

This logic was appealing outside Schaetzel's office as well as in; it appealed particularly to Henry Owen, Walt Rostow's deputy in the Policy Planning Council, whose life was now devoted to a multilateral solution for the nuclear problem in Europe. During 1960, Owen had joined in a summer study with his former boss, Robert Bowie of Harvard, who had headed Policy Planning under Foster Dulles. Their study fathered MLF, a seaborne MRBM force, distinguished by mixed-manning and by multilateral ownership, which Germans could get into but not out of. Owen, helped by Bowie, had pursued this idea from the old Administration to the new, refining and adapting it and meanwhile clearing ground for it wherever he could: the sentences on Britain in the 1961 "Green Book"— • the NSC directive State had cited on September 8—were one among his ground-clearing endeavors. So was the letter which included the citation. Schaetzel's staff had drafted this but Owen had revived it, after long delay occasioned by foot-dragging in other quarters.

The principal opponents of that letter were in Jeffrey Kitchen's Office of Politico-Military Affairs, a general-purpose staff link to Defense which had a tie to Rusk through Alexis Johnson, the Deputy Undersecretary. Kitchen and *his* deputy, Seymour Weiss, did not oppose the policy espoused by Schaetzel's people—the President himself had favored it in speeches—and were not opposed on principle to Owen's nuclear solution. But they disliked the pace and were mistrustful of the timing. Being farther from the British-EEC negotiations they were less inclined than Schaetzel to believe these "must" come off. Being nearer to Defense Department problems-of-the-moment they were more inclined than Owen to respect a bird-in-hand, the Anglo-American relationship. With Johnson's aid—and a weak ally in the British desk—they had held up the Schaetzel draft until it was reduced from "action program" to mere lecture. Even so, they still had been reluctant on September 8.

Now, as they found that SKYBOLT was in jeopardy, the problem Weiss and Kitchen saw was how to *square* the Anglo-American relationship with European policy, sacrificing neither to the other. The problem seemed to them insoluble: compensation for the British was essential, but Tory politics would put the price too high for Europe's comfort. Regarding SKYBOLT, Kitchen's office yearned for the *status quo*.

For all these State Department aides, mid-November was a time of high frustration. They had no leverage on the impending budget decision. Moreover as they now learned, one by one, through Rowen, they would have no place at the negotiating table: McNamara, not Rusk, was to consult the British. Rowen thus was very welcome when he raised with them his study of alternatives. McNamara's interest in alternatives gave them a role to play.

On November 23, the day of McNamara's meeting at Hyannis Port, Rowen met with Owen, Schaetzel, Weiss and Bowie, among others, at the State Department. Bowie, just back from a European trip, was there in his capacity as a part-time consultant. Rowen told the whole group what he previously had told some: the nature of his assignment and the outcome up to now. He reviewed his findings on the four alternatives discussed in Nitze's meeting of November 9. When he reached POLARIS now moved to fourth place, the group exploded. Weiss ventured that this probably was where we would come out. His colleagues, to a man, denounced him for the notion. "You'd have thought," Weiss recalls, "that I'd called Christ an atheist in a room full of bishops."

To Owen and to Schaetzel both, with their converging interests, PO-LARIS risked the whole of European policy for nothing but fidelity to a declining ally whose defense posture was silly on its face. Schaetzel, more than Owen, had some interest in the Tories: we needed them to put EEC membership through Parliament. But not at this expense; this risked their chance to get the membership. From Owen's standpoint it risked more than that: nuclears for Germans.

Bowie, the "consultant"—with the freedom of his status—argued loud and clear that *nothing* need be risked, except the nerve of the two Secretaries and the President. The British should be told that they could lump it. Why offer anything that went a single step beyond what they already had? If they wanted the expense of making SKYBOLT, let them do it. If they wanted HOUND DOG, let them have it. Nothing more. If the government should fall, "let it fall." Labour, once in office, might turn kinder to the EEC and sensible about defense, which would be an improvement. But the Tories, in all likelihood, would *not* fall. They would put on a great drama for our benefit, threatening and pleading, playing alternately on our friendship and our fears. Then, if we stayed firm they would accommodate somehow, without losing their grip on office. All it took was nerve.

Hearing all this, Rowen said that if these were State's views they should be put before Defense officially. He then went home and put his own views to his Secretary. By memorandum, November 23, he gave his findings on the four alternatives. He then drew some conclusions:

> c. If the British choose to continue the SKYBOLT program, they would be charged the appropriate incremental costs. . . .

Nitze's staff, with help from Hitch's office, had been cool to McNamara's first-thoughts of financial aid. Further:

> d. We should offer them the alternative of using HOUND DOG. If it is technically feasible . . . [it] would be a good deal cheaper. . . .

e. We should indicate . . . that they have the alternative of the multilateral force. . . .

To go beyond this to . . . a national sea-borne missile force . . . would signal to NATO that we had abandoned our position of aiding only a multilaterally owned and . . . manned force. . . . If we are prepared to change our policy against bilateral missile arrangements then . . . SKYBOLT might be an occasion. . . . But the crucial decision concerns the basic NATO policy issue—not SKYBOLT.

The "basic NATO policy" he cited had been reaffirmed by Washington in May and June, after two bouts of argument on nuclear assistance to the French, combined with a long wrangle over NATO needs for land-based nuclear missiles. The process of reaffirmation had produced NSC's NSAM-147 in April, McNamara's NATO speech at Athens in May, his public speech at Ann Arbor in June, topped off by Thomas Finletter's statement of June 15, to NAC. Essentially the choices had been negative: not to weaken in pursuit of integration for the West's strategic forces, and not to compromise a build-up for the West's *conventional* forces. Therefore, by action or inaction three decisions followed: *not* to base MRBM's in central Europe, *not* to aid the French, and *not* to back Bowie's idea of MLF in any form which might confer substance on European nuclear status—or divert funds from conventional goals.

If symbolism would suffice, then MLF might do the trick. An American technical mission, the Smith-Lee team, had gone to Europe in October, offering a mixed-manned force of surface ships to carry NATO missiles. Europeans had been told that if *they* wanted this *we* would participate, but it was up to them. Privately, the President and McNamara, among others—not Owen and perhaps not Bundy—had conceived that if the Europeans pondered MLF they might decide the trick was not worth doing. They then might drop the symbols and leave everything to us, which would be better still: the simplest and cheapest form of integration possible, assuring also non-proliferation to the Germans.

The British bomber force, meanwhile, already had been integrated, not in theory but in practice. The two strategic air forces were thoroughly coordinated. No one thought that Britain would assert her "independence." The Anglo-American relationship ran deep.

Nuclear integration and conventional build-up were twin themes of "basic NATO policy" and had been so since the Acheson Report, the "Green Book" of 1961. In 1962 both themes were valued equally by

McNamara, who saw them as two facets of a single purpose, "controlled response" with a variety of "options," conventional defense among them. Rowen's thinking coincided with his Secretary's, though in Rowen's mind conventional options probably came first.

"Basic NATO policy" put Rowen on the side of State, but not for State's reasons. To Bowie and to Owen, the great stake in these "military" matters was political: binding Germany and building "Europe." Britain's "independence" was a major obstacle. To Rowen, on the other hand, the great stake was controlled use of appropriate force in threats of war, or war itself. Britain's "independence" was a minor complication, a problem not of substance but of salesmanship. Their agreement was, in this sense, accidental.

Owen and his colleagues lost no time in formulating State's official views. The next day, November 24, they pressed another "Dear Bob" letter on the Secretary of State. Tyler went along with this, initialed what the others wrote, but stayed above the struggle.

Rusk read, listened, questioned, then returned the letter for technical revision of one point. Some hours later he received a revised version. Its cover note informed him that "DOD staff have emphasized . . . the importance of State making clear directly to Secretary McNamara its views regarding US aid to a UK nationally manned Polaris. . . ." Perhaps the point was not put quite in Rowen's terms. Also, "Mac Bundy has already conveyed to DOD his own opposition to including such aid among SKYBOLT alternatives." Bundy's assistant, Colonel Laurence Legere, had indeed told Rowen that it "would be out of the question from the White House viewpoint."

The letter then was signed by Rusk and sent to McNamara. "In any discussion with the UK," it began, "we should mention these possibilities:"

> 1. British continuation of a SKYBOLT program . . . through a cutback production program in the US. . . .

Nothing was said of financial aid; it seems to have received no thought from State Department aides intent on Europe, scornful of the Tories and anticipating the reactions of Defense Department "budgeteers." Also:

> 2. Use of HOUND DOG on at least some British aircraft. I gather there are various technical problems and uncertainties. . . .

3. Participation in a sea-based MRBM force under multilateral manning and ownership, such as NATO is now discussing. . . .

It seems essential that we make quite clear to the British that there is no possibility of our helping them set up a nationally manned and owned MRBM force.

. . . the difficulties of bringing EEC negotiations to a successful conclusion might be significantly enhanced.

. . . The political costs of our continuing to deny MRBM aid to France would be significantly increased.

The German problem would be even more serious. . . .

Let McNamara consult London to his heart's content. He was now "under instruction."

VI. Thorneycroft Keeps Quiet

London had been on notice since November 9. When we were ready to consult they would be ready to respond; so ran the reasoning in Washington. But this was just what they could *not* do without something more from us; so ran the reasoning in London.

The British Defence Minister had kept his counsel, "no impact," when Zuckerman told him of Hawthorne's word that SKYBOLT cancellation was assured. But by his own account this was no news to Thorneycroft:

I had met Bob McNamara in September. He obviously was not the sort who'd take the trouble to talk with Gore and then call me unless he pretty definitely meant to do something. I saw that at once.

Thorneycroft had also seen that he himself was caught in a cleft stick. On the one side, if Washington "junked" SKYBOLT, so should he; the sooner the better. He wanted no part of *that* brief. His predecessor, Watkinson, and the Prime Minister had taken the position that SKYBOLT certified Anglo-American "interdependence." They had endorsed the weapon, very publicly, as something on which England could rely because America had chosen it, would make it, and would use it. In private they had reasoned, as Watkinson recalls: "If SAC go for it we must have it . . . to maintain the integration of our forces and our joint planning with you." In 1960 this had also been the cheapest course, and had posed fewest problems, bureaucratic or political. The Government had bet on it without reserve; and had done nothing since to hedge the bet. But this, as much as anything, had been a bet on SAC. Now SAC looked like a loser. Who would be the first to pay? The current Defence Minister.

Thorneycroft recalls, "there was no point in flogging a dead horse. One should go on to the next thing." But how? This was the other side of the stick:

> I needed something to step out on next. That is why I mentioned polaris to McNamara. But I could not step out . . . until I was sure I could get it. I had to have that assurance first from the Americans.

He needed our assurance first. He needed it because he could not let his Air Force—or his Navy, or the aviation industry, or Treasury, or the Prime Minister—tag him as favoring POLARIS on *principle*. This was tantamount to treason, selling SKYBOLT down the river. It would make him seem another Zuckerman. He could not advocate a change in everybody else's treasured *status quo* until he could show cause and chart another course. He was not now in position to do either. He could not say aloud what he might privately infer, that SKYBOLT was a dead horse; no *American* had said so, not to him or Gore. Nor could he say that if his colleagues would accept POLARIS as a substitute, he could get it for them; McNamara had listened, not responded. There was nothing for it but to await the response. Meanwhile the less said the better.

Within his Ministry, Thorneycroft kept his mouth shut. He shared his problem with his Private Secretary, Arthur Hockaday; between them they made certain discreet inquiries, "very compartmentalized." But not even Sir Robert Scott, the Permanent Under-Secretary, was taken into confidence "lest it embarrass him to know." Least of all, apparently, was Zuckerman to know; *he* might applaud.

So Thorneycroft recalls. Hockaday backs him up. Superficially, their retrospect seems internally inconsistent. They say he saw at once what Watkinson and the Prime Minister had swept under the rug two years before, and kept there: that Tory defense posture wobbled on a weapon which was marginal for those who had to make it and of dubious utility to them if ever made. We now were drawing a conclusion which had been embedded, like a time-bomb, under British policy since 1960. Seeing this, the Tory Defence Minister sensibly decided to "step out"; so far so good. But why then wait for us to volunteer the stepping-stone? Why not make sure of our intent, by speaking to us plainly?

The answer evidently lies in Thorneycroft's appraisal of his *personal* position, his own stakes, *vis-à-vis* his Ministry and Whitehall as a whole. In terms of personal and bureaucratic politics, silence with his colleagues was the safest course for *him*, and lack of talk to us assured security at home: McNamara–USAF–RAF, or any variant, was a potential channel of communication. Shades of McNamara in September.

Weakness in the Tory *policy* position, as Thorneycroft remembers he perceived it, should have counselled every effort to make sure of *us*. Or so logic suggests. But weakness in his *personal* position, as he evidently felt it, counselled silence everywhere, not least with us. He broke his silence once in a terse conversation on the phone with one man, McNamara. He then made an exception of some sort—not wholly clear—for another, his Prime Minister, of which more later. By all accounts he went no farther, nor did he go back a second time. Michael Cary, the then Acting Cabinet Secretary, comments:

> If he really was aware, or thought he knew in November that you *meant* to cancel SKYBOLT, and that it was politically imperative for us to have you *offer* POLARIS, then it became incumbent on him, as the responsible Minister, to find out why you hadn't offered and to make sure you would do it when McNamara came over.
>
> He should have gone to Admiralty House and said "Prime Minister, we haven't heard anything; we can't afford to have McNamara come here without offering us what we need; I can't be sure he understood me on the phone; will you communicate the necessity to the President or have de Zulueta communicate it to Bundy?"
>
> If what he told you is correct, he failed to do his duty by the PM and the Cabinet.

Thus speaks the civil servant guarding Britain's "Cabinet system." But before one takes his judgment as conclusive, it is well to consider what the Minister, a politician, faced in personal terms. And it is well to recall that Thorneycroft's silence in November rather resembles McNamara's silences before November 9, to say nothing of after. Within their different contexts each man faced internal problems, bureaucratic and political. Each chose to meet his problems in a fashion which precluded frankness with the other. Each took his own convenient, hopeful view about the other as sufficient substitute for direct contact. It must be said for our Secretary that his policy position—and with it his regime's political position—was far *stronger* than their Minister's. He was far less dependent on the other man's performance and had less need to know what that would be. But one may say for Thorneycroft that his personal position was far *weaker* than McNamara's. He was much more dependent on good will from his own side, and ran a greater risk in chancing contact overseas which might reverberate at home. He even ran some risk, as will be seen, in *seeking* contact through his own Prime Minister.

Thorneycroft's problems started with his services. The RAF was utterly devoted to SKYBOLT; that and the V-bombers were its mission and its life. The Army, with its mission on the Rhine, was not competitive and service honor assured that it would not hit the other fellow's vitals. The Navy had its bonds of honor too: one did not take the other's mission—and the money—unless it had been snatched away by Ministers, or by Americans. Besides, POLARIS as a substitute conveyed more threat than promise. With a strategic mission under water, competitive for men and funds, who would be left to show the flag in the Mediterranean? What might happen to the money for new carriers in the Indian Ocean? (Shades of our own Admirals in the later 1940's.) Also, very possibly, to quote another Minister, "The Navy doesn't want to shoot at cities; it wants to shoot at ships"; or anyway at military targets. Add the Chief of Staff, Lord Louis Mountbatten, an Admiral and royal besides, which posed a special problem in a government of Tories.

Another problem specially significant for Tories followed from the RAF's close links with industry. The "military-industrial" complex in aviation, English-style, is less exposed than ours, less "organized," more intimate. But it exists and it extends, reportedly, deep into Westminster, to say nothing of Whitehall.

To the RAF and friends it was no secret in November that SKYBOLT was again on the defensive at the Pentagon. But this had occurred before, specifically the year before and the year before that. The details of those episodes were somewhat cloudy, but results were plain: all had come right. Why should 1962 be different? McNamara, after all, was acting circumspectly; he had put the matter to his Service Chiefs. No one doubted how *they* would advise.

Everybody knew, of course, that the Americans had left themselves an out. The British had accepted it—indeed they had suggested it—when terms were set in 1960. The SKYBOLT Agreement called for an American development if "technically feasible," with a British share to follow, assuming we went on into production. If technically *in*feasible there would be no complaint from British services or Tory back-benches, nor criticism of the government for *trying*. But nothing heard in London had convinced the RAF, or press, or politicians (or technicians) that SKYBOLT's current plight was "technical"; far from it.

In 1962, "cost-effectiveness" was not a term of art known to the British. The Ministry of Defense had no "Hitch counterpart" as yet. McNamara's reasoning was scarcely understood; his words of warning about "cost" and "time" had fallen on deaf ears. "So what?" He had used these words in his last interview with Watkinson, but he had also asked to know British production needs. Watkinson, then on the lookout for assurances, took this for a promise. In September, McNamara had employed those words again with Thorneycroft, but had proceeded to release production funds. If his object was to quiet Air Force fears, he also lulled the British.

Zuckerman, to be sure, among other scientific advisers had been scathing in his comments about SKYBOLT for years past, and warned repeatedly of comparable sentiments across the water. But his very tone and terms—and repetition—misled his non-scientific colleagues. His *bête noire* was the weapon's guidance system; accordingly, his warnings seemed more technical than fiscal. And technically he sounded hypercritical: for British purposes SKYBOLT's "effectiveness" required only that the Soviets should fear it might hit somewhere in a city.

No more was wanted from the weapon than a threat of primary attack which would sustain the British claim to have a nuclear deterrent. That much the RAF, and Douglas Corporation, and technicians on the scene kept promising could be achieved, indeed was now in sight.

In this difference between British purposes and ours lay a great source of leverage which they could use—and later did—to make good their insistence on a substitute from us. For the difference was reflected in the fact that we were now about to cancel our development *on other grounds than what they saw as technical infeasibility*. If "cost effectiveness" was not a term employed in Whitehall during 1962, it also had not been used at Camp David, two years earlier. Nothing on the face of the SKYBOLT Agreement gave a precise forecast of the action we were taking. Our "moral obligation" was bound up with that omission, and the White House session of November 7 shows we knew it. So Thorneycroft inferred from McNamara's phone call. He also inferred that since we knew it we would be forthcoming without leverage. But many of the Minister's associates suspected we knew nothing of the sort. How was he to argue otherwise? By citing our man's words? They could point to different words from the same source.

Thorneycroft's friend "Bob" had "opened up a bad flank" five months earlier. McNamara then had spoken at Ann Arbor and had talked with George Brown. In the course of his commencement speech our Secretary of Defense had characterized other people's national deterrents as strategically irrelevant, unstabilizing, wasteful, and more likely to invite attack than to deter it. Many English journalists and Tories took this personally; the upshot had been a disclaimer by the Secretary with respect to Britain. But in his private talk to Brown, then Labour defense spokesman, McNamara had enlarged upon the theme, alluding quite specifically to British plans for SKYBOLT. Brown lost no time in using what he knew to taunt the Tories. He had attacked them roundly in the House. He did not give his source but it was widely known at Westminster. Watkinson, replying for the Government, had stood on the superiority of Tory judgment and of Whitehall's information. It was a wobbly platform but the best he could produce.

Now, despite Watkinson's departure, an after-taste from that debate remained. So did memories of McNamara's earlier speech-making. Thorneycroft might think that "Bob" meant to do right, but would anyone believe him without some substantiation? On November 9 and after he had none to offer.

Thorneycroft had plenty of incentives to be quiet: all these and two more, the Treasury and the Prime Minister. POLARIS would cost Britain more than SKYBOLT; the Chancellor's reaction was predictable. And SKYBOLT had been chosen by Macmillan. If the choice was faulty then the fault was his. He had done the deal with Eisenhower at Camp David; he had put it through the Cabinet and backed Watkinson in Commons; the weapon had his name on it. Watkinson's successor was well aware of that.

Still, Thorneycroft by his account was quite prepared to "step out on" POLARIS when the time came. Why POLARIS? From his perspective nothing else made sense. To carry on with SKYBOLT would be costly; moreover, he and Hockaday soon found that it would be prohibitive to transfer the development to Britain. For them to contract, independently of Washington, with Douglas Corporation some 6000 miles away was to run risks of strikes, or low priority production, wholly beyond reach of HMG. No Ministry official—to say nothing of the RAF—would have much use for that. As for HOUND DOG, it combined the disadvantages of shorter range with a poor fit for V-bombers. By the time adapting had been done improved defenses might preclude its use. Besides, there was another disadvantage (overwhelming, I suspect): how could a Tory Min-

ister defend the proposition that the national security depended on a
"hound dog"?

For Thorneycroft, POLARIS thus became the only means to meet the
purpose for which SKYBOLT had been chosen by Macmillan: a viable,
politically defensible, and satisfying symbol of Great Britain's standing
in the Nuclear Club.

POLARIS had, besides, distinct advantages. For Thorneycroft it was
more than a substitute; it was, decidedly, a better proposition. The
POLARIS system, submarines and all, assured that symbolism for at least
a decade longer than the SKYBOLT and V-bombers could have done.
Also, it gave the British a far greater gift to bring across the Channel
into Europe.

Thorneycroft believed then—and still does—in Anglo-French nuclear
collaboration as the key to settlement of many things: of Europe's claims
on nuclear status, of French estrangement from NATO, and of Britain's
bid for membership in EEC. Had it been up to him that bid would have
been buttressed by an offer in the nuclear sphere. Macmillan had decided otherwise. The Lord Privy Seal, Edward Heath, recalls:

> Our friends in France had told us that it wouldn't help our case with
> de Gaulle to try to buy our way in. They may have been wrong, but
> that's the assumption on which we proceeded.

Their friends in America had told them something else: that nuclear secrets were not theirs to sell.

Thorneycroft dissented but could not insist. What he could do, however, was visualize an interesting prospect once they did get in. POLARIS
would make it more interesting.

POLARIS in these terms bore no relation to the "odd American idea"
then being offered by the Smith-Lee team: a mixed-manned "multilateral force." British submarines with British missiles spelled an independent deterrent, fit replacement for V-bombers. MLF was something else,
an "extra." Funds for such a force on top of money for POLARIS might
be the straw that broke the Navy's back. Thorneycroft and his colleagues
took at face value Washington's assertion that the Smith-Lee force was
something others should consider, if wanted. They did not want it and
saw nothing to consider. Owen's German problem did not exist for
them; they did not share his premises.

POLARIS was the horse to ride in due course, but not now: time enough when McNamara turned up with an offer. Meanwhile, Thorneycroft kept quiet and did nothing. As a Minister who had his way to make on tricky ground, he could not see that there was anything to do. Contrary to Washington's assumptions and intent, its warning had immobilized the man to whom addressed. But Thorneycroft was not alone in this. That warning also had immobilized Macmillan.

VII. Macmillan Waits

If the Minister of Defence was privately prepared to "step out" when the time came, the Prime Minister was not. At Macmillan's end of Whitehall the warning of November 9 brought rather different motives and perspectives into play. But on a cardinal point these came to the same thing: for the time being there was nothing to be *done*.

On November 11, Thorneycroft sent Admiralty House a summary of McNamara's telephonic message: indefinite warning of a likely possibility with consultation probable before December 10. This was done by formal Minute which the Private Office set alongside Gore's dispatch of November 8. In keeping with his stance of silence Thorneycroft *wrote* no more to his chief; how much more he said to him is not entirely clear. As he recalls, in private conversation with the PM he told "everything": his view of Washington's intention, also Zuckerman's; his thoughts about POLARIS; his hint to McNamara; his assumption that the latter got the point and would produce. The PM's Principal Private Secretary, Timothy Bligh, recalls Macmillan's understanding of the matter in about these terms, and thinks there was a full exchange between them. Another Private Secretary, Philip de Zulueta, is inclined to doubt it. Only Macmillan could settle the point; I did not see him. But whether the Minister said all this or not makes little difference. For according to Macmillan's aides, the PM had sufficient reasons of his own to hold off talk or action on the basis of that phone call.

The Prime Minister had taken office in the aftermath of Suez (Whitehall spells it "Dulles"), with American relations at their worst, British prestige at its lowest, Tory prospects dim. Macmillan personally had worked hard on repairing the American relationship and also on obtaining from America the wherewithal to help him buttress Britain's world position as a nuclear power. Since 1957, these two had been the cardinal points of reference in his foreign policy: the "special relationship" and the "independent deterrent." For him these were at once essential to Great Britain, good for Tories, and adornments of *his* place in history: a powerful conjunction of ideas.

The 1960 meeting at Camp David crowned and symbolized both points. The Camp David communiqué had also mentioned Holy Loch, a Scottish base for the Americans to service their POLARIS submarines. The formal documents had not associated Holy Loch with SKYBOLT; nor had the Americans in public statements. But in Macmillan's mind there was no doubt that he had made a *deal*: the political price he paid at home for Holy Loch matched Eisenhower's budget cost for SKYBOLT. Each alone and both together spelled "interdependence."

Now and for two years past, Macmillan had been inching his way toward a third point of reference for his country, and his party, and his record: British entry into "Europe" *via* EEC. This now was at the crux, still not assured. Until it was assured he wanted to hold tight to what he had. When it was assured he hoped to fit the three together, yielding none. Meanwhile there should be, if he could help it, no agonizing choices posed or taken. Unlike Americans inside our State Department he did *not* view his relationship with us and his deterrent as synonymous; he knew them to be separable. But the last thing he wanted was a separation; that might force a choice between the two. It might even force a choice between America and Europe.

McNamara's warning raised a horrid prospect: Pandora's box might open; those choices might emerge. The issue for Macmillan in November was how to sit on the lid.

The issue wore two faces, transatlantic and domestic. In foreign terms the problem turned on compensation: what is to be the future of "interdependence"? Washington was warning of a change, on its initiative. But the initiator had not offered answers to the question. McNamara had not even said to Gore and Thorneycroft that they could be assured of mutual satisfaction. He had but said he would consult on what they might devise. This was courteous but not forthcoming; it was tantamount to no "offer" at all. What then might the Americans have in their minds? Ann Arbor? Abandoning the spirit of Camp David? Why had Eisenhower's successor said nothing to *him*?

The warning was a puzzle. Thorneycroft had taken it for granted that McNamara's definite intent could not be stated "for some reasons of his own." The Minister assumed these were Defense Department reasons: Air Force relations probably, compounded by that odd phenomenon, Congressional relations. Thorneycroft had also heard the other's tone-

of-voice to mean that "consultation" stood for "compensation" and that
McNamara knew from him what it would have to be. But Admiralty
House was not the Defence Ministry; no tone-of-voice from Washington
had been heard there. Besides, Macmillan's stakes were larger than his
Minister's, and different. The Prime Minister, in caution, could take
none of this for granted.

Macmillan's aides recall that he hoped for the best and made allow-
ances for Washington: Kennedy, of course, had been preoccupied by
Cuba. But in Macmillan's eyes the *status quo* was "best"; therefore he
had to think about the worst. If Kennedy were set to cancel SKYBOLT
would a threatened breach between them be enough to make him keep
it? This, I gather, was the most compelling feature of the transatlantic problem as observed by the PM, never mind how it looked to his
Minister.

In domestic terms the issue at his level had two aspects: Cabinet attitudes and back-bench reactions. The first of these was much the more
significant for the PM. Bligh recalls:

> For several months I think there had been growing an uncrystallized,
> uncanvassed, latent Cabinet sentiment against prolonging the effort
> to sustain the independent deterrent. Butler, our "Prince of Wales for
> 37 years," had never shared the PM's sense of its electoral importance;
> Maudling had little to complain of, so long as the deterrent didn't rise
> in cost, but looking ahead to obsolescing V-bombers. . . . Heath's
> mandate ran to EEC, not nuclears, but certainly he knew they'd be
> around to haunt him, sooner or later. McLeod had been impressed by
> McNamara's logic—Athens and Ann Arbor and the like—and proba-
> bly at heart was for dismantling all deterrents except yours. Boyle and
> Joseph wanted all the money and attention they could get for "wel-
> fare," Tory progress. . . .

The Cabinet had decided two years earlier for SKYBOLT. That remained
the Government's position. Nothing had occurred to force revision of
the *status quo*.

> But if a change had been put to the Cabinet in November, especially
> if it involved more money, all those latent feelings might have crystal-
> lized *against* going on . . . the hell with it.
>   The PM was not unaware of that. . . .

Cary, at the Cabinet Office, has the same recollection, almost word for word.

It is worth noting that of Ministers mentioned, Butler and Maudling were persistent foot-draggers on British entry into EEC. Butler by all accounts was just then stalling agricultural concessions, lack of which had slowed negotiations to a crawl. The PM would not have been altogether "among friends" had SKYBOLT gone to Cabinet in November.

In November there was nothing for the Cabinet to consider. Indefinite warnings do not go there. Had we given definite notice *without* compensation, something would have had to go there. Fortunately we did not. The PM thus was spared one agonizing choice: preserving his deterrent then would have required rallying the Cabinet and his party against *us*. Or had we coupled warnings with an assured compensation which was generous but expensive, this too would have gone there. But we did not do that either, which spared Macmillan quite another agonizing choice. Out of curiosity I asked three Senior Ministers, Maudling, McLeod, and Thorneycroft: "What if we had made a '50-50' offer on remaining SKYBOLT costs in mid-November, instead of five weeks later?" Each answered, "That would have been very complicated for us." The civil servants, Bligh and Cary, were less discreet or more decided: "There'd have been a lot of sentiment, perhaps overwhelming, to let the deterrent go; to carry on alone would have been unattractive and they couldn't have blamed anything on you."

Cabinet decisions once taken are best left alone as long as possible, at least while they embody what the PM wants. "Iffy" propositions are not items for discussion, least of all when the agenda-maker *has* what *he* wants but cannot be sure that others (and the Ministries behind them) still support his view. So it was with SKYBOLT on November 9 and after. Cary recalls: "Nothing much was said except that you Americans were reviewing again and if you thought to make a change we'd be consulted; the Cabinet would be kept advised."

Not only is it best to leave decisions alone, but also it is no light matter to seek new ones. As de Zulueta puts it:

> The PM has it easier with Ministers than with the civil servants. The ranks of civil servants do not work for *him*. They have to be brought along. They are loyal to a "Government Decision" but that takes the form of action in Cabinet, where the great machines are represented by their Ministers.

It may be that the Minister who "represents" effectively in Cabinet, House, and press, or with his interest groups, gains something of a shield against the PM's power of appointment and dismissal. If so, this helps explain why civil servants have a hold on Ministers. At any rate, de Zulueta draws a moral:

> The obverse of our show of monolithic unity behind a Government position when we have one, is slowness, ponderousness, deviousness in approaching a position, getting it taken, getting a "sense of the meeting." Nothing in our system is harder to do, especially if press leaks are at risk. You Americans don't seem to understand that. . . .

Discussion of an "iffy" proposition often will proceed in an informal inner group. But now, regarding SKYBOLT, even this was too much for Macmillan. Such a group could hardly manage without Mountbatten. But he was not a Minister (and possibly no Tory); he might talk to Services, including RAF. If so, the talk would spread. While McNamara's warning remained "iffy" there could be no point in that. And after all, what was there to discuss?

As for back-benchers, the PM evidently felt that if it came to choosing a new line his troops would choke it down, at least while he could put the case in his own terms and time. He was more sanguine than a Gore or than our State Department, 3000 miles away. If Washington made good its warning there would be embarrassment and Labour jeers, no doubt, regardless of the choice. But provided *we* kept quiet until *their* choice had been made, the Government could cope with any hazing in the House. This was, of course, a large proviso. On the plane of press relations the Americans were "security risks." As viewed in November, from Admiralty House, the back-bench problem was a Washington problem.

So was everything else.

On November 15, the PM cabled his Ambassador in Washington. Gore was asked to put three matters of procedure to the President: first, that there should be no press leaks before consultation; second, that there should be no decisions until after consultation; third, that consultation should take place as soon as possible, assuming we proposed to make a change. Macmillan also asked Gore whether, at this juncture, he should have a word with Kennedy directly on their telephone. Gore replied November 21; it took him a week, which is interesting in itself. He

reported that the President was most responsive on the matters of procedure. As for telephoning now, Gore thought it premature: Kennedy had
told him that he had not yet gone deep into the matter and was taking all
the papers with him to Hyannis Port, over Thanksgiving. Before the holiday, therefore, there would be little point in London's call; afterwards,
presumably, Washington would be heard from.

On this understanding, Macmillan did not use the private phone.
With negotiations in the offing he must not appear to press, lest he seem
"weak." The initiative was Kennedy's—not his. The President had chosen to begin at lower levels; let him choose when to move the level up.

Macmillan was not "weak" in personal terms and evidently had no
fear of seeming so. The Profumo case has taught us since what he then
took for granted. His policy position and electoral prospects were on
another footing, also British power relative to ours. Here, indeed, were
weaknesses but these were of a sort which he habitually turned into
strength with *us*. Using weakness as a weapon to assure our acquiescence was S.O.P. for him; the classic technique of the weaker ally. Camp
David evidently is an instance. Nassau was to be another. But this calls
for a certain staging; time becomes important, also scenery, also props.
For him the phone did not appear a proper vehicle, nor was the timing
right, not when the man who should have spoken first had chosen *for
some reason* to employ the author of Ann Arbor as his spokesman.

If Macmillan were to save the *status quo*, he could not trust us to preserve it for him as a private favor on his private urging from a distance
of 3000 miles when he was heard, not seen. He could not trust us because our behavior indicated either that we meant to do him mischief—
which he doubted—or that this was no light matter in our minds. Like
Thorneycroft, the PM evidently did not think a McNamara would take
trouble without reason. Macmillan *got* the point of McNamara's call
which is why *he* forebore to telephone once Gore, who knew the President far better than he did, advised delay. With that advice to buttress
McNamara's warning, an uninvited phone call seemed no way to make
the President keep SKYBOLT. But the PM meant to make him keep it if
he could.

In Washington the question still arises, "Why didn't he call us?" In
London, not long ago, Macmillan talked to Henry Brandon more
bluntly than his staff to me, putting the same question with some bite—
and in reverse.

While Kennedy proceeded to Hyannis Port, Macmillan took the news

of the November by-elections on which Tories had been banking to
show good results from his "purge" in July, his "new face" for the Party.
There were six of these November 22. The results were far from happy.
All six elections disappointed Party hopes and cast new doubts on Tory
standing with "swing" voters. There soon was back-bench grumbling
that the "new face" was not new enough.

Macmillan now had a new weapon in his hands to use with us. Unfortunately, he would soon see still another ally, who did not view Tory
weakness as a strength.

In the post-election atmosphere Macmillan waited for some word
from Washington. None came. Messages went back and forth on other
subjects, but not SKYBOLT. On November 27, Admiralty House and the
White House announced a meeting of the President and the Prime Minister in Nassau three weeks hence, December 18. The meeting had been
pending for some time as one among their semi-annual "get togethers."
On these Macmillan doted as a sign of their relationship. Now the date
was set for three days after an engagement to see his prospective partner
in the EEC, de Gaulle. The meeting with the French was not expected to
be easy; Macmillan had looked forward to relaxing with Americans. But
by November 27, with nothing heard from Washington, he took it that
SKYBOLT would be the main business of Nassau. His aide de Zulueta
had not made this point to Bundy when they settled the arrangements.
From his side what could he say?

Not until December 3 did London hear that Washington was ready
to consult; McNamara would see Thorneycroft December 11. On December 12 both men were scheduled to arrive in Paris for a NATO min
isterial meeting. Macmillan was to meet de Gaulle December 15. At
Admiralty House no one supposed that McNamara's one-day stand,
in this progression, could conclude the SKYBOLT case. Nassau necessarily remained the place for that. But there was hope of clarification;
waiting was about to end. McNamara's visit would show Washington's
intentions.

VIII. December Interlude

Our Secretary of Defense had not deliberately delayed his trip to London. At Hyannis Port, November 23, when he got his decision he had
thought to go the next week, well before December 10, the outside date

that he had given Thorneycroft. This evidently was the thought in everybody's mind at the decision-making meeting.

The President, so far as I can find, said nothing at Hyannis Port about
his words with Gore on "matters of procedure." Evidently he saw nothing to be said. Those procedures were implicit when he first had talked
with Rusk and McNamara on November 7; thus it had been easy to ac-
cede to Gore's request. Everything done since seemed in accord with
that request. Consultation in a week would be more of the same.

But the next week was a busy one for McNamara. He was readying
other chapters of his budget which had piled up as a consequence of
Cuba; he was about to deal with New Delhi's requests for aid. Also he
had scheduled on November 30 an interagency "defense policy conference," a preview of December's NATO meeting. For a variety of reasons, the Smith-Lee team among them, he did not want to miss that
conference.

So McNamara did not go before November 30; afterwards the NATO
meeting loomed so close that it appeared "a waste" to lose a day from
work and make two trips instead of one. Accordingly, he rolled the two
together and decided to see Thorneycroft *en route* to Paris: hence his
request, December 3, that they should meet in London on December 11.

In the process two things slipped from sight: Macmillan had sought
no publicity before decision and no Decisions before consultation. The
President had promised both, though perhaps no one else knew that,
and both were consistent with the Secretary's earlier assurances to
Thorneycroft. The action at Hyannis Port did not seem inconsistent (to
Americans) since it had been declared "subject to consultation," and
since there had been no publicity. But the workings of the budget process would transform that action into formal—well nigh irreversible—
Decision at the moment when the Services were notified.

Such was the logic of McNamara's "probable leak date" December 10, estimated early in November. His estimate was off by three days.
On December 4 Hitch notified the Services that SKYBOLT was eliminated
from the budget; current programs would be cancelled at the end of the
month; in the interim there should be no disclosures. On December 7
authoritative news stories, implying cancellation, appeared in the *New
York Times* and the *Washington Post*.

McNamara's trip was still four days away.

Had McNamara known what Thorneycroft was thinking, or Macmillan, or how their thoughts diverged, or had he even known how little

they were *doing*, no doubt he would have used his own time rather differently in the days after November 23. But he knew none of this. The British evidently had absorbed his warning calmly, more calmly than Gore. Nothing to the contrary was heard from their Ambassador, or from our own man Bruce. Indeed, nothing was heard at all about London's reaction. Silence probably amounted to assent; no news probably was good news. So it seemed to McNamara, hard at work.

Why did he learn nothing from the British Ambassador? Gore was no nearer London than he; for all Gore knew there had been *no* reaction, excepting the Prime Minister's concern about "procedures" which at most implied a waiting game. What Thorneycroft could not tell his own Permanent Secretary he did not confide to cables aimed at Gore. What Macmillan would not say to Cabinet Ministers he did not put in Foreign Office messages. From where Gore sat it looked as though his Government "had stuck its head in the sand." Lacking information or instructions he took it as his task to report all he could and to prepare the ground as best he could for a solution, when and as his ostriches should want it.

Gore worked in the dark; to complicate his lack of word from home, he evidently did not grasp the processes and politics of Hitch's defense budgeting. Early in December Gore and Gilpatric discussed the proposition that we keep SKYBOLT afloat from month to month, while EEC negotiations clarified and by-election fall-out subsided. Gilpatric was encouraging, so it seemed to Gore, but the idea got short shrift in the Pentagon. From where Hitch sat, continuation this year and elimination next was nonsense as a matter of Congressional presentation and would arm proponents of the program. To postpone elimination would be worse, if possible; to start the session justifying something when one knew that later one would seek the opposite, broke every canon of effective budgeting and risked the whole stake in the President's decision: $2.5 billion.

To Gore this still seems a "parochial" concern; in programmatic terms, however, it had overtones of life-and-death, much like Macmillan's concern with his Cabinet. Both were "parochial" in the same sense and both became decisive. Gore is not the sole Ambassador, nor his the only Foreign Service to find such behavior puzzling when practiced by foreigners.

As for Bruce in London, he might have learned what Gore could not: he was on easy terms with Thorneycroft and the PM; he might have

asked and they might then have hinted what they thought. But Bruce
had been immobilized in the same way as they: by the terms of his message from McNamara.

The cable Bruce received November 12 was the first in his memory
which had reached him "Eyes Only" from another Secretary than Rusk
through channels other than the State Department's. Did this mean Mc-
Namara wanted State kept in the dark? Was security involved? or feud-
ing? Was Rusk fully informed? If so why had there been no word from
him? McNamara's cable did not ask Bruce to *do* anything; it coupled
non-instruction with the information that direct talks had begun and
would proceed at ministerial level. What might Bruce be doing if he got
into that act? In prudence he stayed out of it.

One of Bruce's aides, Raymond Courtney, his "Politico-Military"
Officer, was sufficiently concerned to draft a cable which Bruce signed
after some thought and sent through "their" Department, State, to
McNamara on November 21:

> . . . If a decision to discontinue . . . the SKYBOLT program is taken . . .
> or seems likely, I believe the Government here should be afforded
> maximum amount of time possible to make its own consequent
> decisions and to prepare its plans and their presentation. . . .
> [SKYBOLT] abandonment now could have the most fundamental
> consequences. . . .

But this told State and Pentagon—and White House—nothing they had
not heard three weeks earlier from Courtney's fellow-FSO's, the BNA
desk officers in Washington.

Courtney might as well have been in Washington for all he knew of
London's inner thoughts. *He* could not deal with Ministers. Unless he
had been intimate with Thorneycroft's Private Secretary, he could have
learned nothing from inside the Defence Ministry. Unless he had been
very close to members of the PM's staff he could not have learned anything elsewhere. And Courtney—like most of his colleagues in our
Embassy—was not the sort of person to whom senior civil servants in
sensitive positions volunteer the private thoughts of principals. The inner politics of the bureaucracy in Britain is not studied by our Mission
there. Nor are its members men with whom their British counterparts
(outside the Foreign Office) feel professional affinity, trade intimate
"shop talk." Bruce would not, Courtney could not penetrate the minds

of a Macmillan or a Thorneycroft. So there was nothing further that our Embassy could offer. What was offered was no use to Washington.

Had Washington *requested* more—through State Department channels or by telephone perhaps—the Embassy's combined resources, mobilized and focussed, probably sufficed for an informative result. Volunteering was another matter.

The lack of word from London may not have bothered McNamara but it did disturb some of his aides. Brown recalls that as November drew to a close, "it made me nervous that we hadn't heard anything about what they were planning; how their considerations were going—when I had time to think of it, that is, which wasn't often." Rowen recalls that on November 28, concerned about the time-table, he suggested to the Secretary that if his own trip were delayed, Nitze and Rubel go as an advance party. McNamara's reply: "I'll take care of it." Rowen took the hint and turned to other things.

This interchange occurred as Rowen handed in a memorandum supplementing his report of November 23. Where SKYBOLT was concerned that finished his assignment. The Secretary's comment told him that he did not have a new one. No one else did either: in finishing his own, Rowen had finished Nitze's. The Secretary handed out no more. Concerned or not, his aides left it at that. SKYBOLT was *his* pigeon at *his* option. They were busy men. And their concern did not run very deep. In Rowen's terms:

> I knew Polaris was possible but I assumed there probably was some way to make the British accept one of the three alternatives. I assumed McNamara could and would shove one of them down their throats— probably Hound Dog. Since that was good enough for SAC it ought to do for them. Anyway, it wasn't my responsibility. I did ask Nitze now and then when the Secretary was going and why the delay. Paul professed ignorance and, clearly, he didn't have the responsibility either. Meanwhile, we had lots to do.

If Pentagon concern was limited, White House concern was almost non-existent. On November 27, when Nassau was announced, SKYBOLT was not even envisaged as a subject; McNamara would have got it settled by then. The man who had just got the bombers out of Cuba certainly could do *that*. Neither he nor Rusk was slated for the trip to the Bahamas; McNamara had a holiday in mind and Rusk would dine the

Diplomatic Corps. Nassau was to be a *pro forma* affair; friendly talk and symbolism for the PM's pleasure, no negotiations. So Bundy recalls.

Bundy also recalls a certain nervousness, akin to Brown's, about the timing not the substance of McNamara's consultation. He called the Secretary more than once to urge against delay. The answer he received was much like Rowen's.

At State, meanwhile, there still were a few active worriers. Weiss and Kitchen, doubtful about the "instruction" of November 24 and fearful London would have none of it, kept searching for a way back toward the *status quo*. Like Gore they sought it in a budgetary accommodation. On November 30 they wrote Rusk urging him to get SKYBOLT continued through a subsidy for British development, thus echoing an early McNamara thought. The thought sat well with Rusk, whose mind was moving in the same direction. But in the sequence of events their advice was a bit belated. It would have served better a week before.

Elsewhere in the State Department, other issues crowded SKYBOLT almost out of mind. As Tyler puts it:

> One absolute priority displaced another absolute priority. The NATO meeting was the thing we had to work on in the last week of November and the start of December.

He and Schaetzel and their aides proceeded to do that. Owen went back to planning: provided McNamara followed his instructions everything would be all right.

At the "defense policy conference," November 30, a free-associating "seminar" which mingled all the ranks, these people gathered with their principals, the President excepted. SKYBOLT was not much discussed. Reportedly, Rusk wished aloud that we had renamed Hound Dog "Skybolt B," and McNamara rejoined, "Dean, you'd have been *great* in the automobile business." McNamara later voiced the thought that sales of US missiles without warheads might be one alternative. Rusk, the minutes note, "did not like" it.

They and their associates then turned to talk of NATO force requirements. The Secretary of Defense pursued a favorite theme: the need for larger European contributions of conventional forces. At one point he suggested that if Europeans were insistent about nuclear status-symbols we underwrite all costs of MLF and free their funds for serious business, conventional forces. This led to running, intermittent argument abut the nature of our policy toward MLF. McNamara lectured Schaetzel on the non-committal cast of our support for the idea and for the Smith-Lee team, implying that somebody was over-enthusiastic. The Secretary spoke with confidence; he thought he knew both Rusk's mind and the President's. But Schaetzel seemed impervious, Owen looked undaunted, Rusk and Bundy were not to be drawn. Discussion wandered on; no one returned to SKYBOLT.

Such inattention did not last for long. That conference coincided with a wave of transatlantic press reports which shortly shoved the SKYBOLT issue back into the minds of men at White House, Pentagon and State.

The press began to get into the act November 28. That day Lord Beaverbrook's *Daily Express* treated London to a front page piece which declared SKYBOLT in danger from a State Department "lobby" trying to strike down the British independent deterrent. (My "spies" report the source of this was George Brown, his tongue in cheek, intent on making trouble for the Tories.) This same day the Air Minister announced in Commons that "it remains our policy to push forward the development of SKYBOLT." The next day, November 29, Washington announced the fifth successive failure of a flight-test. On November 30, the *Daily Telegraph* conveyed reports from Washington that work would go forward despite failures: ". . . no present intention of scrapping SKYBOLT." On December 2, however, Brandon wrote from there that anti-SKYBOLT men were "now in the ascendancy." Then, December 7, came the authoritative hints of SKYBOLT's demise. These brought a rash of reactions in the British press, the stronger for a sad coincidence: on December 5 Dean Acheson had lectured at West Point.

The Prime Minister himself spoke in the House to answer Acheson's alleged denigration of Great Britain. It was an emotional performance. Beneath the scorn for Acheson there lay a mounting worry at the lack of official word from Washington on SKYBOLT.

On December 10, McNamara and Rusk met the President and Bundy at the White House, once again, for final talks before the Secretaries went their ways to NATO: Rusk direct to Paris, McNamara *via* London. Just before the President came in, Rusk queried his colleague on the possibilities of subsidizing British efforts to continue the development of SKYBOLT. Rusk had been thinking of his three approved alternatives; the more he thought about them the more he saw a need to "sweeten the pill." McNamara told him that by various devices we certainly could shoulder some remaining costs, if Britain chose to carry on development. (Financial aid had been in his own mind as early as November 9; their staffs had let it drop while framing those alternatives.) He told Rusk he would pursue the matter the next day, if need be, when he saw Thorneycroft. The President then joined them.

Bundy's notes record that with respect to Britain and the three approved alternatives:

> Mr. McNamara did not believe that the British would be pleased by any one of [the] alternatives. . . . What he thought we might consider, at some stage in the negotiations, was a proposal to give the British access to a more up-to-date weapons system on the condition that the venture become multilateral if and when a multilateral force should be developed. Such a course might conceivably be taken, for example, with Polaris.

As time would show, "multilateral" in this context was not identical with MLF to McNamara or his auditors. Further:

> The Secretary of State, while not disagreeing . . . indicated his own deep concern with the difficulties that would be posed for the British by a cancellation of Skybolt. He appeared to incline toward a major effort to assist them in meeting the remaining development costs, so . . . they would at least have a fair shot at obtaining what they'd been counting on. . . .
>   The President indicated his general approval of Secretary McNamara's proposal, and said he was not eager to join in a large share of further development costs for a weapon to be supplied only to the British. . . .

This conversation bears comparison with Rusk's "instruction," Rowen's conclusion, Legere's statement on "the White House viewpoint" three weeks earlier. Rusk had been supportive of his aides in their presence. McNamara had been silent with his own, "I'll take care of it." Legere spoke for whom? Apparently for part of Bundy's undecided mind. Nothing in the record represented what the Secretaries and the President now said to one another.

Even this conversation scarcely represents, in full, what McNamara evidently thought. POLARIS had been in his mind from the beginning; SKYBOLT, once discarded, looked more dubious each week, not only for himself but for an ally. When he received Rowen's report and Rusk's instructions he had faced a choice. As he recalls, he made it deliberately (and has regretted it since):

> I never thought State's three alternatives contained a viable solution. I thought I ought to give them a run for their money in case I was wrong. But I never did think the British were likely to buy any of them and I never thought for a moment that if the British didn't buy them, we could leave it at that. I thought we'd probably end by giving them Polaris. I'd said that on November 7 and Mac had agreed. The President and Dean hadn't disagreed.
>
> But my own people were dubious and Rusk's people were dead against it. I thought he wanted me to give them a crack at what *they* wanted. I decided I might just as well do that. . . .

Rather than precipitate a row with his associates, he meant to let the British press POLARIS on him. And so he flew to London to meet Thorneycroft, who had precisely the same notion in reverse.

IX. McNamara Meets Thorneycroft

On the morning of December 11, as he arrived in London, our Secretary of Defense made a short statement to the British press:

> Mr. Thorneycroft and I will have a full discussion. . . . One of the things we are going to talk about . . . is the Skybolt program. . . . In Washington . . . we are taking a very hard look at all of our programs. This includes Skybolt . . . it is a very expensive program and technically extremely complex. It is no secret that all five flight tests attempted so far have failed and program costs have climbed sharply. . . .

When this statement hit the streets, early that afternoon, there was considerable shock in Whitehall and at Westminster. The American was denigrating SKYBOLT before consultation even had begun. From the safety of Schweppes, Watkinson for one was outraged; he recalls, "If I'd still been in office I'd have refused to see him." Thorneycroft, however, remained calm. He was at the airport and he heard the statement made. As he recalls, he thought it a bit "premature" but possibly quite useful since that afternoon he was to get an offer of POLARIS. McNamara's attitude was no surprise to Thorneycroft; he felt no shock. His turn was soon to come.

Thorneycroft went off to Cabinet on the understanding that they would meet after lunch. McNamara lunched with the assistants he had brought along, Nitze and Rubel. When they left to meet the Minister, McNamara commented, as Rubel recalls:

> I've got a card up my sleeve but I'm going to let them play it: we give them Polaris on the understanding they assign their subs to NATO. I think that's where we're going to come out. I'll start with my three options, then I think they'll ask for this.

Shortly after, they assembled in Thorneycroft's office with the Minister and several senior Ministry officials. McNamara opened by distributing copies of an *Aide Memoire* which gave the grounds for SKYBOLT cancellation and presented the three State Department alternatives. He then read the whole document aloud. Thorneycroft remembers "ruffling through the pages" looking for the word "POLARIS." He found it only in conjunction with the adjectives "mixed-manned" and "multilateral," Smith-Lee no less, in Thorneycroft's phrase "a non-starter . . . no relevance to this matter at all . . . nothing to do with a substitute for SKYBOLT as a means of maintaining our independent deterrent."

The discovery left him "profoundly shocked."

Ever since November 9 Thorneycroft had calculated that POLARIS must be brought to him; he could not go for it. He could not be seen by Englishmen "to plead on my knees with Americans." Nor had he wanted

> . . . to be seen by my people in the Services, in the House, or in the press, to be locked in a struggle with Bob McNamara for SKYBOLT . . . a struggle where I would fail to beat him.

Even if the outcome were POLARIS it would then be tagged in public as a "sop," a "second-best," a "defeat." (So it later was.) Now to his surprise he faced the absolute necessity of choosing one of these appearances. The Secretary's morning press statement deprived him of all chance to duck the choice. Did he want to look a pleader or a loser?

It took Thorneycroft no time at all to make that choice: better valiant than craven. While the other still was reading he decided on his course. In Hockaday's phrase, "he had to move back to Square One." The moment McNamara finished reading, Thorneycroft proceeded to do that.

He spoke emphatically but slowly; Rubel, fascinated, took verbatim
notes:

> I won't comment on the technical judgments. . . . I am confident that
> your experts have advised you as you have indicated in your paper.
> I am equally confident that other experts could be found to argue the
> other side.
>
> I will discuss the political implications. This missile is at the heart of
> British defence policy. It is the key to the continuing of the V-bomber
> force. It is the only example of complementarity between the U.S. and
> Great Britain.
>
> Moreover, the SKYBOLT project arose as part of the context and
> complex of other decisions. We made the U.K. a target by agreeing to
> base POLARIS at Holy Loch. That agreement and the SKYBOLT agree-
> ment were both taken in the same context.
>
> A decision to cancel the SKYBOLT would not only have grievous po-
> litical consequences to me and to my party. It would not only be seized
> by the opposition for that purpose. . . .
>
> We, on our side, of course, always said you would never let us
> down. We had to say that because we put our reliance in you abso-
> lutely. Now they will be able to say that they were right and we were
> wrong. . . .
>
> Moreover, the position is made harder by recent statements by
> American spokesmen concerning the independent British deterrent.
> A number of U.S. spokesmen have made themselves heard on this
> subject recently. Even your speech at Ann Arbor, Bob. . . . the British
> press, and many others will say the SKYBOLT decision is part of that
> policy. They will say this decision is really taken to force Britain
> out of having an independent nuclear deterrent. The recent speech
> by Mr. Acheson will be seized upon to place this action in that
> context. . . .
>
> And so, Bob, I would like to ask you a question. If you are going to
> cancel the project, are you going to say that it won't work, or are you
> going to say that it will cost too much?

McNamara answered candidly, "We won't say that it is impossible,
but we will say that technical problems dominate the decision. . . ."
Thorneycroft rejoined:

> Of course, but most missiles slip their schedules. Most of these proj-
> ects cost more. . . . Many of them are less accurate than they might

be desired to be. But to cancel this project tears the heart out of our relations. . . .

The Secretary then attempted to proceed to practicalities: "Would you continue the SKYBOLT project alone if we did cancel it?" The Minister snapped back, "That is the only interesting alternative." Hearing this, McNamara told him, "We'll certainly make it as easy as we can for you to take that alternative. . . ." There followed some discussion of ways and means. Then Thorneycroft returned them to another level:

Of course, Bob, this matter . . . really relates to the political factors. These dominate. It really concerns the interpretation that is going to be placed upon this action. The opposition is bound to say that your real reason for cancelling the SKYBOLT is to end this relationship and to change the posture of Britain. . . . What do you say to that?

"Bob" did as best he could: "Well, I'd say that we have spent and we are spending a lot of money to keep you in the position of having an independent nuclear deterrent. . . ." This naturally was not enough for Thorneycroft. He put the question in a harder form:

Assuming that you were to cancel SKYBOLT, would you be prepared to state publicly that the United States is willing to do everything possible to assist Britain to keep its independent nuclear deterrent?

McNamara answered: "Yes, I would. Of course, we would have to consider Germany, France and, for that matter, you and your commitments to the Common Market." But Thorneycroft was having none of that: "If you would support us publicly, we're not worried about the Common Market." McNamara tried another tack, "We could do that in the framework of our willingness to let you continue the project." Thorneycroft shot back, "I'm talking of policy." To which McNamara responded: "But the best evidence of policy is specifics, such as our willingness to support SKYBOLT until you take it over." (They were talking different languages; "policy" to Thorneycroft meant symbols, not "specifics.")

The Minister then got down to cases, point by point:

Yes, but how can we realistically expect to do that? . . . We have cancelled other projects, we have made ourselves absolutely dependent upon you. . . . Besides, we can't really afford to take the project over in any case. . . .

None of these alternatives that are set forth in the paper are viable. The . . . cost [for SKYBOLT] would be excessive. . . .

We'd never consider the HOUND DOG. . . .

I am the greatest multilateralist of all. . . . But after I have my forces, not before. It is easy for you to favor multilateral arrangements. . . .

And finally,

I notice you've dropped POLARIS from your paper. We talked about POLARIS on the telephone, why have you dropped it?

McNamara evidently pricked up his ears. After saying he did not recall such talk, he put a question: ". . . . Would you buy POLARIS systems if we could make them available?" Some discussion followed and then Thorneycroft inquired, "Why is furnishing POLARIS a problem to you?" Again McNamara did the best he could: "Well, there are legal problems, especially with respect to the nuclear parts of the submarine such as the reactor. . . ."

Zuckerman then tried to change the subject:

. . . if most experts feel that SKYBOLT is no good it really wouldn't make very much sense for the U.K. to support it. If the U.S. decides that that's why SKYBOLT should be dropped, then the U.K. shouldn't pick it up.

McNamara quickly—perhaps gratefully—tossed that ball back:

The public should not be misled by our statements. We have kept it up only because of the British interest in it. You, Solly, have always known this. Your other experts have always known it too.

But Thorneycroft was not to be diverted:

No, the question goes beyond SKYBOLT or the problems of SKYBOLT. The decisions were all taken in context. We had SKYBOLT and you had the POLARIS berthing at Holy Loch. You must go out of the decision on SKYBOLT, if you do, with another decision that is taken at the same time.

That other decision must be a positive one—namely the decision to publicly specify that the U.S. supports the British independent deterrent.

Nitze recalls that at about this point "I asked Thorneycroft if they had considered the effect upon their relations to the Common Market of the UK acquiring an independent POLARIS force. Thorneycroft said that first of all this was a matter for them to worry about and not for us to concern ourselves with, and secondly that

> de Gaulle would have no legitimate grounds for complaint. After all, de Gaulle was the man arguing most loudly for a national deterrent.

Discussion then turned for a while to submarine programs on which the Minister did not seem well-informed. "At that point," Rubel notes, "Mr. McNamara proposed the alternative that he had indicated before the meeting he hoped the British would advance on their own:

> Would you consider saying that after you got your own POLARIS submarine force you would make it part of a multilateral force?

Thorneycroft responded strongly:

> Not as a condition upon us. After the announcement and the decision, then the UK can go into multilateral arrangements just as the US can. But the UK must enter any such arrangement as an independent power. No matter what the savings in cost might be, we have no option except to go that way.

Nitze then asked about the possibility of an Anglo-American collaborative operational arrangement. He mentioned the manner in which both strategic air forces coordinated plans. Thorneycroft replied:

> Yes, we could make collaborative arrangements of that kind. Are these forces operable on their own? That is the test. We have no objection to integrated operations, but there must be the *possibility* of separate even if degraded operations.

The meeting recessed on that note.

If Thorneycroft was shocked by McNamara's *Aide Memoire*, the latter was "appalled" by Thorneycroft's response. The accusatory lecturing left McNamara unmoved; as Nitze recalls, "he took it like a tank being spattered with eggs." But the Minister's lack of precision on costs, his unconcern for, even ignorance of problems in adapting his own submarine program, these things disturbed the Secretary deeply. Rubel's notes record that when discussion turned to British submarine designs and time-schedules in case these should become POLARIS carriers:

> It was not clear to what extent the UK had given this or any related matter much consideration. . . . Solly revealed that they had a single sheet of paper on which they had written down their thoughts. Insofar as I was able to discover this was the only document in his possession or anybody else's, concerning this matter.

In McNamara's recollection of the meeting:

> They hadn't done their homework.
>   They hadn't done a thing. They had made no plans. . . . They obviously hadn't given any thought to what would be satisfactory for them and how to get it and how to present it publicly. . . . I'd given them a perfectly good warning and it was obvious they'd made no use of it. . . .

McNamara had not done *his* "homework" either; when it came to POLARIS he brought nothing to read. But Thorneycroft's state seemed quite unlike his own, at least to him.

This impression shocked the Secretary of Defense but he was soon to have a stronger shock. He dined with the Minister and carried on into the evening. Then when they adjourned he saw the evening papers. He was featured in them all as a man who had assaulted British interests but had been stood off by Thorneycroft in a "tempestuous" meeting. Britain's Defence Minister "had made it plain to Mr. McNamara that cancellation of the SKYBOLT project would lead to complete reappraisal of British policy and defence commitments." According to "Defence Ministry spokesmen," Britain had "counted on the SKYBOLT as its chief deterrent weapon," had counted, indeed, on the United States and McNamara had been "left under no illusions as to the consequences of . . . cancellation."

The Secretary took it that these stories had been written in the Ministry. There probably was no need for that. Hockaday recalls:

> After McNamara's statement in the morning all the press needed to know was that he hadn't offered satisfactory alternatives. All it took

to know *that* was the lack of better word. We had no good news to pass along. There was no need to write their stories . . . and no way to stop them either.

Maybe so, but McNamara read them as deliberate, slanted leaks. What was Thorneycroft trying to do? Maybe he really meant to turn anti-American. The thought trailed the Americans to Paris the next morning.

Thorneycroft went off to Paris on another plane pursued by other thoughts: Why hadn't McNamara said "O.K."? Maybe "they" really meant to strike down his deterrent. If so, what would become of it, and him?

For both these men the flight was short, but not relaxing.

X. Flap in the Ranks

On Wednesday, December 12, a large part of official Washington assembled in Paris: Rusk and McNamara, Tyler and Nitze, Rostow, Schaetzel and Rowen, among others. A portion of official London was there too, notably Thorneycroft and the Foreign Secretary, Lord Home. Macmillan stayed behind, but not for long. On Saturday morning he was to meet de Gaulle at the Chateau of Rambouillet. Kennedy remained on his side of the Atlantic. Macmillan was to meet *him* the next Tuesday.

For six days echoes of the McNamara-Thorneycroft exchange reverberated in Paris, London, Washington and Rambouillet. On the seventh day came Nassau.

The news that McNamara brought from London split the Americans in Paris. He and Rusk agreed at once that they wanted no crisis in Anglo-American relations. The formula would have to be about what he had thought: POLARIS with some sort of NATO link, if possible, to symbolize "multilateral" and to signify "integration." This squared with Nitze's thinking on bilateral relationships, "spokes in a wheel," and his concern lest Britain slide toward neutralism. Rowen, when he heard the news, thought no more than "Oh hell, so they've got it." But Rostow, Schaetzel and assorted others, whose eyes were fixed on EEC or MLF or both, dissented vigorously, almost frantically against that formula.

Rusk bore the brunt of their reaction; the dissenters were his people. Our Ambassador, Charles Bohlen, gave a dinner where the host and virtually all the guests united to assault the Secretary of State for putting British wants ahead of European purposes. In everybody's view but his he valued our relationship with Britain much too high. By all accounts their vigor finally ruffled his composure: "What do you want of me and the President?" he reportedly demanded, "we have to have *somebody* to talk to in the world . . . we can't talk to de Gaulle . . . or Adenauer; do you want to take Macmillan away and leave us nobody?. . ."

The next day, in a staff meeting, Rusk revealed more of his views. As one distressed subordinate then told a friend in Washington by "Dictabelt":

> . . . The Secretary said he wasn't against the special relationship until he could see something better to take its place. . . . The Secretary said categorically he was not concerned about the possibility of a German [nuclear] program, stating that the Germans were committed under the Brussels Agreements and that any change on the Germans' part would constitute a radical change in their relations with us and he didn't think they would take it. . . .

The dictation continued:

> Obviously . . . if the US is not concerned about the possibility of a German program or of diffusion in general, we are on a wrong wicket. . . .
> . . . . However, I don't make too much of this since, as you know, Foreign Ministers are assailed with a multitude of problems during NATO meetings and the purpose of our session with the Secretary was merely to report the facts to him, not to try to get any decision. . . .

Rusk might take a stand regardless of his aides, and so might McNamara with a cheer from Nitze, but between them they could not commit their government to anything until they got to Washington and saw the President. Meanwhile, Home and Thorneycroft were close at hand and asking; there was nothing the Americans could answer.

This left the Englishmen less comfortable than ever, and Thorneycroft for his part more inclined than ever to suspect a plot. He may have talked then to Pierre Messmer, his French colleague, about a scheme for nuclear collaboration (they certainly talked later). However that may be, he did unquestionably pace the floor with Home. A British Embassy official vividly recalls the two of them, "marching up and down the room saying to one another, 'Will they give it to us?' and 'My God, if they don't the Government might fall.'"

Back home their Cabinet colleagues were "in shock," confronting this new trouble suddenly, on top of others which already had unsettled many Tories: scandals in security (the Vassall case), November's by-elections, Katanga—and Rhodesia—and two months of Cabinet agonizing over agricultural concessions to the EEC. The PM, for his own part, contemplated Rambouillet and Nassau, just ahead.

In Washington, meanwhile, rump groups at State and Pentagon worked under Bundy's urging on the problem now exposed by McNamara's "consultation." A fairly good account of his exchange with Thorneycroft reached Washington from Courtney on December 12. So did press reports. These demonstrated that November's three alternatives would not suffice to meet "the British problem." Courtney's cable did not manage to convey with Thorneycroft's full force that the heart of *their* problem was *our* generosity, and that we were "generous" *only* if we backed their "independence." It told enough, however, to put the President on Bundy's back and Bundy on the phone with the Departments, calling for a fresh alternative.

The Pentagon reaction was straightforward: irritation at the lack of British planning, anger at the charge that we had shirked our obligations, and a willingness to let them have POLARIS as a substitute if that was what they wanted and were now prepared to pay for. Cooperation between Navies could be just as between Air Forces. Regarding NATO ties, there had been no prerequisite where SKYBOLT was concerned, so need be none with a straight substitution. The alternative of going on with SKYBOLT as a subsidized British project was considered and discarded; why throw good money after bad? These were the premises on which staff work proceeded under Gilpatric's aegis between Wednesday and Sunday when McNamara returned.

In State the premises were altogether different. George Ball, the Undersecretary, had been following the SKYBOLT question only since the first week in December; Schaetzel, formerly his own assistant, then had brought it forcibly to his attention. But Ball was deeply, personally committed to EEC, to British entry, to United Europe *à la* Jean Monnet. His connection with Monnet ran back without a break to Lend Lease days. Ball had not regularly followed nuclear issues, but United Europe set him against national forces, disposed him toward Bowie's view and Owen's, whenever his attention was engaged. Once he got into SKYBOLT his reaction, though more flexible and more considerate of Britain's plight, did not differ essentially from theirs.

Before McNamara went to London, Ball had told Gilpatric that we must not seem to have decided first and then consulted. He had urged

McNamara to say nothing to the British press. Now that his advice had been ignored, so it appeared, he was to cope with what he naturally regarded as the consequences.

In that frame of mind Ball conferred off and on for days with his available associates, among them Bruce who had reached Washington *en route* to Nassau, Bowie along with Owen, Johnson, Kitchen and Weiss. The theme of every session was the same: the thinking at Defense must be reversed; a "substitution" of POLARIS must not happen. After failing to help France, opposing land-based missiles, offering MLF, we dare not signal Europe that we would discriminate afresh in London's favor— especially not now with Britain still outside the EEC, and especially not POLARIS with submarines more glamorous than Smith-Lee surface ships.

What to do? Notions of all sorts were canvassed. There was much re-ploughing of old ground: SKYBOLT, HOUND DOG, MLF. Bowie at one point contributed a new thought, an Anglo-American joint study, to buy time. Others circled back to putting prices on POLARIS, terms of NATO or of MLF commitment. Weiss in desperation went the whole way back to calling for reversal of the SKYBOLT budget decision.

Tyler, fresh from Paris, arrived on the fifth day of these proceedings. They astonished him. With his ear as sensitive as ever, he had left France feeling that the issue was essentially decided. He found his colleagues talking as though what he just lived through was the future, not the past. Their discussion seemed to him unreal:

> It was something like going under water. Here they were, pursuing the issue with enormous passion, as though they could affect what had already happened . . . I had been at lunch with Rusk and all our people when McNamara flew in from London. Before the meal was over one could tell how this was ultimately going to come out. . . . Here they were in Washington still passionate, with Rostow and Schaetzel, who had been there, coming back to reinforce them. It was curious.

Other returning travellers did not share this perception. Schaetzel came home full of gloom and fight. Rostow arrived bursting with ideas; like Ball he had got into the act late, it still intrigued him. He brought home copies of his two most recent memoranda, both of which had gone to Rusk and now reached all the others. These proposed that we distinguish sharply between aid to bomber and to missile forces (an old idea of Kaysen's, once considered for the French). While bombers lasted we could help national forces, with offers for de Gaulle as well as Britain. It was not very clear what our assistance would entail: the choices ranged from HOUND DOG with B-52's attached, to further study. Regardless, as we offered aid and got our friends to take it we could bargain on the line that they stop short of surface missiles and accept a multilateral arrangement for that stage.

Rostow's shortness on specifics tossed the ball to others, but his drawing of a line, his stress on bargaining, his mention of the French, appear to have left traces in the minds of some among his readers.

While the McNamara-Thorneycroft exchange set off these noises at Defense and State, its airing by the British press drew notice from another part of Washington. On Saturday, December 15, a long lead editorial in the *Washington Post* commented acidly:

> Weaknesses of Skybolt as a weapon are less alarming and less disappointing than the weaknesses in the conduct of American foreign policy. . . .
>
> . . . the Government of the United States has handled its relations with Great Britain with little consideration for British feelings, and not much evidence of real concern about the British position.
>
> The two countries entered into a mutual agreement to develop Skybolt. That agreement led Great Britain to abandon the Blue Streak and make the Skybolt the basis of the country's thermo-nuclear power. . . . the United States should have developed an alternative proposal for maintaining Great Britain's thermo-nuclear capability, and for preserving that nation's air arm. With this alternative in hand, American officials of highest level should have taken the matter directly to British counterparts.
>
> . . . .
>
> Instead of this, the United States Government, disclosing its inherent misconception of the nature and gravity of the crisis, dispatched its able Secretary of Defense to England. . . . But this is not solely a weapons problem and it is alarming to see that this Administration is handling it as though it were.
>
> Having begun the Skybolt matter as awkwardly as possible there seems now a grim determination to stick to precedent and carry through at the same fumbling level. Prime Minister Macmillan and Foreign Minister Home will journey to Nassau. . . . The Secretary of State cannot go because he is entertaining the Diplomatic Corps. . . . He may go down in history as "the man who went to dinner". . . .
>
> . . . The British are feeling ill-used. . . .

. . . If we don't respond as a friend ought to respond to that feeling, their emotions will be justified and fears about the adequacy of the State Department confirmed.

Rusk was the ostensible target, but the White House knew at whom the *Post* was shooting.

On Sunday, December 16, the Secretary of Defense returned and went straight to a meeting with the President. Gilpatric brought a delegation from the Pentagon. Ball brought some of his discussants. Rusk was absent; he had stopped in Lisbon. Bundy's notes record:

. . . McNamara indicated his opinion that we could consider selling [Britain] the Polaris missile. . . .

. . . Ball expressed his concern. . . . any [such] arrangement . . . would lead us at once to the question of what we would do to the French, and so inexorably, to the question of . . . the Germans. . . .

. . . The President pointed out that in the eyes of the British there could well be a claim that the cancellation of Skybolt implied some obligation to provide a substitute, on our part. "Looking at it from their point of view, which they do almost better than anybody," he said, "it might well appear to them that since Skybolt was a substitute for Blue Streak, which they had cancelled on our assurances, we should now provide an alternative.". . .

To say nothing of the eyes of Britain's friends in the United States, including a Republican named Eisenhower.

Their outlook was not mentioned but reportedly it was much in the President's mind. The Publisher of the *Washington Post*, in a personal call, had brought it forcibly to his attention. So had press reports with London datelines. How would our bipartisan Establishment react if *Britain* charged us with dishonoring an *Eisenhower* obligation? What would become of that articulate "elite" support for European policy which Democratic Presidents had nurtured since the War? What of the board-rooms of the *Post*, the *Times*, *Newsweek*, *Time-Life*, and CBS? What of their influential readers and viewers? Was Kennedy risking his membership card in the Council on Foreign Relations?

Bundy's notes continue:

. . . McNamara argued strongly that . . . our current position with respect to a multilateral force simply will not work . . . the Europeans

[will not] buy and pay for both a multilateral force and . . . NATO
conventional force goals. . . .

. . . Ball . . . told the President that this might be the biggest decision he was called upon to make. The President's reply was, "That we
get every week, George." Yet the President clearly recognized . . .
grave political risks for Mr. Macmillan and serious risks also for our
own policy in Europe. . . .

. . . further discussion . . . led the President to approve, for planning
purposes, the following general proposal:

1. We would offer appropriate components of Polaris . . . to the
British
2. . . . the British would commit their eventual Polaris force to a
multilateral or a multinational force in NATO
3. . . . the British would undertake to build up their conventional
forces . . .
4. The terms governing the use of SKYBOLT would apply also to . . .
Polaris. . . .

. . . . This conclusion was much influenced by the advice of . . .
Bruce that since we had told the world we would not help national . . .
forces, we should relate any assistance in this field of MRBM's, to a
large-scale solution of the broad problem of the Atlantic deterrent. . . .

This conclusion was *not* influenced by Thorneycroft's advice that item
two made item one no substitute for him, no answer to our "obligation." Bundy's notes do not suggest that anybody dwelt on this. No one
present had *heard* Thorneycroft except McNamara. No one asked for
Nitze's testimony, or Rubel's.

Curiously, it was only in the course of this meeting that McNamara's
staff discovered he had been under some misapprehension about the
original SKYBOLT Agreement. He evidently had thought it provided for
NATO assignment of the missile-bearing V-bombers; his proposition
on POLARIS thus may have appeared to him straight substitution. His
assistant Adam Yarmolinsky, who had spent the past week making
himself master of the files—including Eisenhower's own Camp David
files—hastened to correct him. The correction did not change the
present issue.

Having got this far, the President left planning to the others for a
day while he did other things. Among these was a "year-end" television
interview with three Washington correspondents. This was released

on Monday, December 17. In his response to questions, the President looked cogent and collected. One question dealt with an advertisement for SKYBOLT which the Douglas Corporation had placed in the American (and British) press. The President replied:

> . . . I saw that ad today. The only thing that we ought to point out is we are talking about two and a half billion dollars to build a weapon to hang on our B-52's, when we already have billions invested in Polaris, and Minuteman. . . . I would say when we start to talk about the mega-tonnage we could bring into a nuclear war, we are talking about annihilation. How many times do you have to hit a target with nuclear weapons? That is why when we are talking about spending this $2.5 billion, we don't think that we are going to get $2.5 billion worth of national security. . . .

The next day McNamara and the President met Rusk, now home again, for a last word before they went to Nassau while he remained behind. (Despite the pleadings of assorted aides the Secretary of State declined to cancel his engagements with the Diplomatic Corps.) The three men met alone. As Rusk recalls, the main thing they discussed was Yarmolinsky's file-research and its inadequacy as a test of what they owed Macmillan. No matter how the documents might read, the British would believe that at Camp David there had been a deal and in the circumstances this was not unreasonable. The preceding Sunday evening Bundy had declared in guarded terms on "Meet the Press" that we had no "fixed obligation." "Fixed" or not, these three accepted it as real.

With this in mind the President emplaned for Nassau.

XI. Macmillan Meets de Gaulle

While Washington was churning, the Prime Minister of Britain spent a miserable week-end. It rained at Rambouillet but weather was the least of it. In spreading chill, de Gaulle outdid the rain.

Macmillan and de Gaulle had last met six months earlier, at Champs. The weather and the atmosphere were then more promising. By all accounts the PM had convinced the General that he really was determined to come into "Europe," accepting its political potential, acknowledging the consequences for the Commonwealth. Besides, he had displayed awareness of the contrast between French and British stakes in agriculture; he had cited labor-force percentages, 20 to 5. Also, he had touched on military cooperation: he had alluded to their two nuclear forces, and had spoken of contingency planning for joint use in cases where America might choose to stand aside. This seems a far cry from Thorneycroft's "collaboration," but not meaningless.

De Gaulle may or may not have been delighted, but reportedly he was impressed. If the British were so European-minded, France alone could hardly keep them out. If they were so determined, they were bound to get in.

But six months is a long time; many things had happened after Champs.

In France, Algerian Independence Day had come and been accepted. In Brussels, Britain had allowed the tempo of negotiations to fall off and seemed more eager to unravel hard-won deals among the Six than to accept their agricultural arrangements. British tactics screened protracted Cabinet efforts to choke those arrangements down. But Europeans, like Americans, believe in the efficiency of English decision-making, so the atmosphere at Brussels had grown cooler than before. In Germany there had been cheers for de Gaulle in September. There also had been the "Spiegel Affair." One outcome was to put the Chancellor on term. Adenauer now, his own time running out, had become eager, anxious for the signs and symbols of a Franco-German reconciliation; Britain counted less, France more.

In England, meanwhile, Macmillan had got into trouble. Never mind intent, what of his capability? Anthony Eden had come to Paris in October and had talked of Tory opposition to the EEC; as a British Embassy aide puts it, "he plunged his knife into the PM's back at every opportunity." Hugh Gaitskell had come over in November and had talked of Labour Party opposition; if the Tories took his country in, a Labour Government might well get out. To underscore these views there came the by-elections of November 22.

And in France three days later, on November 25, de Gaulle quite unexpectedly had won a startling victory in Assembly elections. His personal party now was as securely in control of the French legislative branch as he of the executive. Adenauer might become a supplicant, Macmillan might be weakening, but he was vastly stronger than before.

When Macmillan went to Rambouillet, he had not added up the past in such a way; his host apparently had done just that, and had drawn a conclusion. At their first meeting, Saturday, de Gaulle did everything but say that he would veto British membership in EEC. He did not speak of "veto"; he was patronizing, not threatening. But he discoursed at length on every conceivable obstacle to British entry, and he left no doubt that in his mind these would prove overwhelming. Britain, sad to say, was just not ready to join Europe, and Europe was unable to absorb a foreign body. He went so far as to suggest that Britain would be well advised to drop her case for membership and seek "association."

Macmillan was astonished, also angry. The next day, for the first time in their relations, he insisted on speaking through an interpreter. He wanted his response to be entirely understood and wanted to use English where a nuance might be missed. This may not have been helpful. When the PM turned to English the General, pridefully, kept hurrying the interpreter and fussed him in the process.

The Prime Minister's rejoinder, Sunday morning, was devoted in the main to refutation point by point, of what he had been told the day before. He argued Britain's European-ness on de Gaulle's terms, and it is not of record that the General was impressed.

In the process of asserting his good faith, the PM touched on SKY-BOLT. He spoke in English, carefully. The British do not know how he was heard, but what he said appears almost *verbatim* in their minutes. He told de Gaulle that as the General knew, his nuclear deterrent was dependent upon SKYBOLT. The Americans were now in doubt about the weapon and might cancel, having other alternatives. If they did so he would try at Nassau to obtain POLARIS in its stead. If he did not succeed in that, then he would have to develop his *own* alternative. To do so might well mean curtailing many other elements in British military forces. He wished de Gaulle to know this as a possibility. If it eventuated he would keep the French informed.

De Gaulle acknowledged the receipt of information and showed no displeasure. He later made a favorable allusion to Anglo-French cooperation on the "Concorde" supersonic transport. But if this was a signal, as French sources later claimed, the British did not see it so and doubt that he did either. "Concorde" cooperation then and since involved two separate national establishments. If it had any pattern-setting relevance in nuclear terms, this ran along the lines the PM had laid down at Champs. In British eyes, de Gaulle and they had always been agreed that a Great Nation should have *national* forces; in this they were Gaullist and he a Tory. Macmillan now had told him that Great Britain was determined to proceed on the same course as France, if necessary by French means: going it alone. The General's silence signified assent, his

"Concorde" reference signified a two-force future. So Macmillan evidently thought then and still does, Parisian rumors to the contrary notwithstanding.

There had been amicable *tête-à-têtes* at Champs, not so at Rambouillet. When the two men were finished with their formal talks they had no more to say to one another. Macmillan left for England with his mind made up on one thing: as he arrived in London he was overheard to say, "I'm damned if I'll go there again."

On Sunday afternoon, de Zulueta wrote up minutes. Over night the British Embassy in Paris pondered them. On Monday morning Cabinet Ministers—and Private Secretaries—read them with attention. Reactions were nearly unanimous. Embassy officials agreed, to a man, that there could be only one meaning: de Gaulle was going to keep them out of EEC. After hesitation about telling the PM what he presumably had heard, the Embassy dispatched its view to London. There, at least outside the Foreign Office, most readers agreed. With the relative detachment of Great George Street, one of the Chancellor's Secretaries recalls, "we knew at once, of course, that it was all over." And at Admiralty House Bligh recalls, "only a bloody fool would have thought we had a chance after that."

But Bligh was Private Secretary not Prime Minister, a leading civil servant not a governing politician. For Macmillan it was not so simple. On the one hand, as Heath recalls, "we were getting split appraisals at the Foreign Office; it did not look as black in Brussels as in Paris, and Paris had been wrong before." On the other hand, and more importantly, Macmillan—and Heath also—had too much at stake to quit until the whistle blew. No matter what de Gaulle might think or plan, the game was not yet over; there were other, independent players on *his* side, the Five, also the Eurocrats. And on the British side there remained tricks to play, notably the long-sought agricultural concessions. From his corner of the Private Office de Zulueta comments:

> When one is in a negotiation one simply cannot know how it will come out until it is over; to conclude prematurely that one is bound to lose, is to disarm one's self. The PM, characteristically, is very much aware of that. His stance as a negotiator is never to let down until the bell, and never above all to *show* that one is giving up. . . .
>
> De Gaulle had never been *friendly*; at Rambouillet he was merely *colder*, but that's relative. He had changed his tack before, he might again. Besides there were the Five. No matter, the worse it looked for

us the *more* important to give him the sense that we were going on, straight on, despite him; as long and as far as we could. To let him sense anything else would have been to play into his hands.

Bligh concurs, and adds:

This put the PM in a special difficulty with you. He could not very well risk press leaks from your side that he had told *Americans* the *French* were going to do us in. That *really* would have torn it. De Gaulle would have had more fun with that than with POLARIS.

Besides, and more importantly, the PM had a *prior* problem, a *different* negotiation, never mind the other. Regardless of de Gaulle and EEC, he now must go to Kennedy for SKYBOLT or POLARIS.

With this next on his list, he spent a busy Monday and then flew to meet the President at Nassau. Home accompanied him. So did Duncan Sandys, a former Defence Minister, now Commonwealth Secretary and reputed "tough boy" in the Cabinet. Aid for India was on the agenda, also perhaps toughness.

Thorneycroft trailed behind; he first put in a long day at the House. SKYBOLT was debated there that Monday. As he had foreseen, Labour jeered, Brown crowed. "We told you so." As he had also foreseen, Tory rightists *rallied* to the Government on grounds of British honor and perfidious America. Sir Arthur Vere Harvey, "Colonel Blimp" in our time, upheld the Minister for fighting the Americans. Thorneycroft once wanted to avoid the role; now he had to play it for whatever it was worth. To give their team a boost 103 Tory Members signed a motion calling on the Government to safeguard their deterrent. Armed with this the Minister, in his turn, flew to Nassau.

There, the PM's party learned from an American reporter of the President's TV remarks concerning SKYBOLT. Kennedy was still in Washington; reporters had preceded him. After a frantic scramble, Macmillan's aides obtained a text to put before their chief. The PM then discovered that his *status quo* was wrecked beyond repair. Finally and decisively, from his own point of view, the weapon's reputation had been ruined. There now was nothing for it but POLARIS. Reluctantly Macmillan put aside all thought of reversing the President on SKYBOLT. The question that his Ministers had asked themselves in Paris now—and only now—became the *sole* question for him: "Will they give it to us?" His aides report that he was far from sure "they" would.

By all accounts the PM's mood was grumpy when he drove to the air-port to welcome the President.

XII. Kennedy Meets Macmillan

The Presidential party which emplaned for Nassau included the British Ambassador as well as key Americans: McNamara, Nitze, Ball, Tyler, Bruce, and Bundy. Once the plane was in the air and headed south, the President invited Gore to join him for a chat.

Then for the first time, as he recalls, the President got to the heart of the British problem, saw beneath the surface of "disaster" for the Tories to the point that there were but two ways for them to ward it off: by hailing our generosity or by assailing our bad faith. The "British prob-lem" was *his* problem; he held the key to *their* resolution. As Thorney-croft had pointed out to McNamara, they needed our support in *public* for the "independence" of their deterrent. That was "generosity"; all else was "bad faith." The point was pure politics, not policy, not strat-egy, not diplomacy, not cost.

The President had been hearing, up to now, from his administrators and diplomatists; he had not quite got the point before. But he and Gore conversed as politicians. In thirty minutes they devised a neat political response: we would drop SKYBOLT as a weapon for ourselves but *we* would carry on *development* jointly with the British, splitting costs between us, 50-50, so that they could get what they had said they wanted. Rusk once came close to this on grounds of honor and obliga-tion; McNamara once approached it but his people had backed off on grounds of cost-effectiveness. The President now seized it, and refined it, "50-50," as a way to square our foreign policy with Tory politics.

What Weiss and Kitchen once had thought could not be done, the President and Gore worked out (on paper) five weeks later in a spare half-hour. The formula was obviously *generous*; it blocked off any charges of bad faith; yet it kept Britain's deterrent on the right side of the line between bombers and missiles, no European complications in that. And although generous to a fault, it raised the monetary cost of "independence" to the British, which might hasten a rethinking of their whole deterrent posture. As a political device for squaring our wants with their needs to our advantage, the 50-50 formula was very nearly perfect. Politically it had only two flaws. First, it cost *us* money. Eight days before, with McNamara and Rusk, the President had jibed at that.

Now he was instructed by *events*. But second, as he and Gore soon
found, they were too late.

When their plane arrived at Nassau they discovered this at once. After
the airport ceremonies, Gore drove off with the PM. A brief exchange
sufficed to notify Macmillan that, as he had supposed, the President
could be backed off some way from cancellation. But Gore found out, in
turn, that the PM had lost taste for any SKYBOLT deal; he now assumed
the posture Thorneycroft had held; he now wanted POLARIS. That evening, Macmillan took the President for a walk and told him so.

Before that walk, the President learned of another conversation during the journey down. Late in the afternoon, he happened to ask Tyler
how the situation looked to him. Tyler responded with the substance of
what he and Ball had discussed on the plane some hours earlier. Tyler
then had written Ball a note:

> George, I recommend that our objective at this meeting be to gain
> time. . . . I recommend the Pres. and the PM agree to the setting up
> immediately of a joint study group responsible to Pres. and PM. . . .
> this group could be directed to report recommendations on a substi-
> tute for Skybolt not later than Jan. 15 or 20 (UK Parliament recon-
> venes end Jan. 1963). . . .

Ball, who had heard of this before, from Bowie, was encouraging.
Tyler put it to the President; Ball seconded. The President had it in mind
when he went walking with Macmillan. Whether he then passed it to
the PM is not clear.

While they were walking, and for hours after, Gore was engaged in
"sitting on" Thorneycroft. If the PM now was bent upon POLARIS, the
original enthusiast for that approach was more concerned about his
stance as fighter of Americans. Thorneycroft, by all accounts, preferred
a breach with us to any settlement which might suggest that he had lost
his battle. The atmosphere inside the British delegation spurred him on.
Brandon recalls this as the angriest delegation in any Anglo-American
"summit" since the War: "The only counterpart is feeling after Suez, but
then there was no 'confrontation.'"

Thorneycroft wanted to leave in a huff, rally the country, go it alone,
and "let you take the fall-out," as an associate later put it. Gore, with
Home supporting, argued hard. He pointed out as he recalls, that "if we
try to claim that the Americans have let us down, they will publicize
their 50-50 offer, which they'd have every right to do. . . . Once publi-

cized, we wouldn't be able to sustain the claim at home that they are against our deterrent. The offer will show that's false. It's a fair offer." Gore got support from an unexpected quarter; Duncan Sandys acknowledged the force of his argument. The offer, Sandys thought, was as much as they had a right to expect. That comment, Gore recalls, "deflated" Thorneycroft. Thus the 50-50 offer was of use that night, even though the PM had refused it out of hand.

The next morning, Wednesday, December 19, the PM and the President, with delegations present, met for formal talks. Whatever they had said the night before, they now were talking for the record.

The Prime Minister began by recounting a history of Anglo-American nuclear collaboration from the war years through Camp David "interdependence" to the present. He said he thought the other allies understood that Washington and London were a "founding company" in nuclear affairs with an historical "special-relationship." POLARIS as a substitute for SKYBOLT merely would sustain it, not depart from it. Why should the allies object to that? As for EEC negotiations, these were separate and apart, wholly unconnected. The negotiations would succeed or fail over agriculture. The effects of an agreement on POLARIS would be "frankly, absolutely none." Regarding multilateral arrangements in the nuclear sphere, national forces would continue side by side with any joint ones, pending supranational political authority. There was no escaping that, and France would scarcely disagree. Allied misunderstanding did not seem to him a problem.

The President, when his turn came, reviewed history from his side, and then posed the 50-50 offer. Macmillan declined it bluntly, "the girl" had been "violated" in a public place. The President argued without much force. He knew what the response would be; besides his Secretary of Defense had no enthusiasm for the thing, and showed it. As Bligh recalls, "McNamara was a splendid chap; he sat there saying 'Balls.'" In McNamara's own terms, as he later put it, the 50-50 offer "was not intellectually respectable except as a last resort"; cost argued against it, so did the product, and so did British contracting with our producer 6000 miles away. But public relations quite sufficed for the PM; he said "no" without reference to these other arguments.

The President had also surfaced Tyler's scheme, proposing a joint study of solutions for the British after SKYBOLT. With supportive interventions from Ball, he countered the Macmillan claim of Allied acquiescence if there were to be decision at this juncture for POLARIS. He spoke of warnings from Ambassadors (he had heard from Bohlen and from others as well as Bruce). He invoked nuclear stands to which his Government was wedded very publicly: non-proliferation, multilateral solutions, no aid for the French. He and Ball between them brought up Germany.

The PM would have none of it. He and Home dismissed the German problem out of hand. The Germans had learned from Hitler. He then turned to attack the issue frontally. His words were a demand for our immediate agreement on POLARIS.

The President now got the treatment McNamara had received from Thorneycroft, eight days before, in still more vivid form with the Prime Minister's full weight behind it. Bundy's notes record the PM's peroration:

> Churchill had told him in 1940 that in logic it was impossible to win the war, but they had gone on. There were lots of people in Britain who would like to chuck it, which would enable them to have better pensions and a more satisfactory life. The . . . alternative [to a POLARIS agreement] was to say this is a complicated system—The Americans won't give it to us—we will go and make it eventually and be free. This would be better than putting a British sailor aboard ship to have tea with the Portuguese. To give up would mean that Britain was not the nation that had gone through its previous history. We should consider that if the people who wanted to give up in Britain came to power, who would make the better ally? Those were the ones we were supporting in Britain by our policies. It was true that Germany was dangerous, but not as much as before the war, because the whole balance had changed and there were now two super powers. Either Britain must stay in the nuclear club or he would resign and we would have a permanent series of Gaitskells.
>
> He would not engage in anything petty. We could stay at Holy Loch. . . . Britain could make submarines —not nuclear ones—to carry missiles. This could be accomplished . . . but the costs would have to be compensated elsewhere. . . . They would have to tax their people more as well. Such a course would lead to a deep rift with the United States. He said he would not accuse America. . . .

In the midst of this statement, Macmillan inserted one sentence:

> He would be prepared to put in [to NATO] all of his part of a Polaris force provided the Queen had the ultimate power and right to draw back in case of a dire emergency similar to 1940.

Now everything was on the table.

Why did Macmillan spurn "joint study"? Why did he fire all his guns for a decision *now*? The answer may be that he found himself engaged in two-front war; Thorneycroft was listening as well as Kennedy. More significant, perhaps, is Bligh's recollection:

> The PM pressed Kennedy out of fear that if he didn't get a concrete offer at this juncture he would never get it later. If he went for a joint study, and another meeting, there would be no POLARIS at the end of the road. Macmillan felt this because of Kennedy's own attitude: he was obviously reluctant to let loose of POLARIS in a bilateral deal with us. It was plain in his whole tone and manner that he didn't want to do it, didn't think he ought to do it. We all sensed that.
>
> Back-bench rebellion had nothing to do with it. That began *after* Nassau. There was rumbling before, but it was anti-American, not anti-Macmillan. The howl afterwards was raised by press reports which got it wrong and called the outcome a "defeat." If we'd taken a joint study instead, he wouldn't have been any worse off afterwards, and maybe better, provided he could have passed the word in private that you'd be generous when the study was done.
>
> It wasn't the back-benchers but policy, and perhaps *election* politics, that he had on his mind. He thought the deterrent was good for the country, and he'd better try to get it then and there.

So the "playing on our friendship and our fears" which Bowie had predicted came to pass in a more formidable fashion than he, perhaps, had thought about when he advised reliance upon Presidential "nerve." The President now faced an impassioned older man embodying a valued weaker ally, who invoked in his own person a magnificent war record, an historic friendship, and a claim upon our honor—in Eisenhower's name—to say nothing of one politician's feeling for another. McNamara and Thorneycroft had spoken different languages; these two spoke the same.

All these ingredients were mixed into the PM's peroration. Macmillan evidently had *not* put them there in conscious calculation of the other man's psychology. As Bligh recalls,

> He was not being tricky, nor was he making a cool calculation of the Kennedy psychology. He was simply making the strongest pitch he could, making the best effort in his power, mustering all the arguments he could think of. . . .

If the President had responded "I'm sorry but I can't . . . ," the PM wouldn't have taken to drink, or resigned or anything. He'd have gone on to face the situation as it then presented itself, feeling that he'd done the very best he could—and able to point out to Thorneycroft, an attentive witness, that he *had* done the best there was to do.

If Kennedy had said those words the PM would be sitting in office yet, just as he is now. . . .

With this view of the proceedings, Bligh himself "sat on the window ledge and waited for the President to say 'Prime Minister, I'm sorry. . . .' The words never came." To have expected them marks the detachment of a Senior Civil Servant, which perhaps is not unlike that of a Harvard Professor.

Whatever else the President may have thought, one thing no doubt was plain to him, that the chiefs of *our* Government, McNamara, Rusk, and he himself, had never been disposed to withhold an agreement on POLARIS if there were no other way to meet the British problem. Three days earlier, December 16, he had cleared for planning purposes a British POLARIS force assigned to NATO. He since had seen two more attractive schemes. Macmillan had rejected these but would accept the other as a new phase of "*inter*dependence," provided he could get one modification: an escape-clause which preserved the precious symbolism of his "*in*dependence." The President was not prepared to balk at that proviso. Instead he turned attention to its terms, and to what Britain could do for us in response.

There followed a succession of informal talks and formal meetings, focussed on the words in which agreement should be couched. The extent of our concession to the British and the character of their response were worked out in the guise of drafting a communiqué. Policy discussion in the act of choosing words, negotiation in the act of swapping drafts, were hasty, improvised affairs. Besides, "there were so few of us," as Tyler puts it. And those few did not include the working draftsmen of our prior pronouncements on nuclear affairs.

For Owen and his colleagues "multilateral" was a term of art, now signifying nothing but "Smith-Lee." Our men at Nassau used it interchangeably with "multinational," and thought exclusively of submarines. The pain this caused in State need not be described. The British, though, were pleased. It had been quite a shock to find that we insisted on a "multilateral" solution. It was quite a relief to find that we encompassed in the term a NATO assignment of national forces. With this they were prepared to live, once they had their escape-clause. They even were prepared to be forthcoming. Macmillan offered to begin the move toward broad, allied solutions, by putting his V-bombers "into NATO" at once. It later turned out that their notion of assignment was so loose as to be useless in our eyes, but at the time this seemed a real return for our concession. He also offered to collaborate with us in further exploration of a mixed-manned force so that nations (Germans) without national deterrents might obtain a voice in NATO nuclear affairs.

Here was a change of front in British views on MLF, or so it then appeared. Together with the gesture on V-bombers, and a bow to conventional forces, this comprised their *quid pro quo* for an escape-clause. We took them up on it and made our deal.

A "Statement on Nuclear Defense Systems" was jointly drafted for issuance as part of the Communiqué. It read:

> . . . The President and the Prime Minister agreed that POLARIS must be considered in the widest context . . . an opportunity for . . . new and closer arrangements . . . of strategic Western defense. . . .

> 6) The Prime Minister suggested . . . a start be made by subscribing to NATO some part of the forces already in existence. This could include allocation . . . from United Kingdom Bomber command. . . . assigned as part of a NATO nuclear force. . . .

> 7) Returning to Polaris [they] agreed that the purpose of their two governments with respect to the provisions of Polaris missiles must be the development of a multilateral NATO nuclear force in the closest consultation with other NATO allies. They will use their best endeavors to this end.

> 8) Accordingly, [they] agreed that the U.S. will make available . . . Polaris missiles (less warheads). . . . British forces . . . under this plan will be assigned and targeted . . . as the forces described in paragraph 6.

> These forces, and at least equal U.S. forces, would be made available for inclusion in a NATO multilateral nuclear force. . . . except where H.M.G. may decide that supreme national interests are at stake, these British forces will be used for the purposes of . . . The Western Alliance in all circumstances.

This language made explicit our agreement to supply them with POLARIS. Not wholly undeliberately, it left the larger issues less than clear.

What was a "NATO multilateral nuclear force" in which their submarines and *ours* would be "included"? Expanded forces under Paragraph 6? An adaptation of "Smith-Lee"? A combination? Time and other governments would have to tell. Meanwhile, neither of *these* governments tied its prestige to any single answer. So both Chiefs of Government seem to have thought. Both were satisfied to have it so. Both wished to know what time would show before they got "committed."

This was a subtle outcome, ambiguities were purposeful. The purpose was protection for each government's prestige in launching an untested, improvised initiative with Frenchmen, Germans, and assorted others. Bruce, a spectator at these proceedings, whose own views were unambiguous, later commented:

> Macmillan was so pleased to have done better than he feared he
> would, a victory in his eyes, that we could have got anything we
> wanted out of him, even an MLF commitment on the spot, if only
> we'd known *what* we wanted. . . .

Not having planned to give them an escape-clause, we were unprepared to name our price and improvised accordingly. This has depressed Bruce ever since, along with many others. But that improvisation does not account, altogether, for the lack of specificity in what we told the world. As events would disclose, the President and the Prime Minister alike had more at stake than trades between themselves; they had at stake what they could "sell" to others, an unknown. While they explored it they were loath to buy a peddler's license in the coin of their prestige. They would have shied away from this, presumably, no matter what their offers to each other.

Judging from what he later said to others, the President understood that very well. Bundy also may have understood it, then or later. Not so most of their colleagues at Nassau or in Washington. Why should they? Others mostly read into the words of the Communiqué a *license* for whatever product *they* wanted to sell. Interpretations were as varied as the policy perspectives of a Nitze and an Owen. Thus "Nassau" helped to set the stage for still another story, "MLF."

While the Communiqué was being put in final form, the PM asked for time to consult his Cabinet; he could act only with their approval. Rather reluctantly, the President agreed to wait a day. Thereupon, Macmillan cabled their agreement to the Deputy Prime Minister in London, asking a reply within four hours of receipt as an accommodation to the waiting President. Strictly speaking, the Prime Minister was under less restraint than this suggests; flanked by Home, Sandys, and Thorneycroft, he could have *told* London, not "consulted." But "form" in English governing has very real importance; "non-arbitrariness" secures Prime Ministers against a host of troubles, as Eden found when he did otherwise on Suez. Even Winston Churchill at the height of his personal power was punctilious about the forms of "collective responsibility"; he always consulted his colleagues. Macmillan was disposed to do no less. He had no doubt of their response: with the key members at Nassau and four hours to reply, the "rump" in London scarcely could demur, and did not do so.

The Cabinet's reply was acquiescent. Enthusiasm, though, was far from high. Cary recalls:

> Left to their own devices, the Cabinet at home would rather have seen Nassau conclude with a joint-study of what should be done after Skybolt cancellation—and then another meeting. Kennedy's proposal would have been acceptable. Members at home weren't pressing for an immediate decision; they were, indeed, dubious about taking *this* decision without further study. Had they been allowed even as much as 24 hours for their doubts to crystallize they might have cabled a preference for joint-study back to the PM.
>
> Butler and McLeod weren't sold on the deterrent; Maudling was concerned about the money; so was Boyle. Heath was terribly worried about Brussels. . . . Mountbatten, whose views would have been heard had time allowed, was scornful about going on with Skybolt, but he also was unprepared for and unhappy about Polaris. . . .

But time did not allow for second thoughts, even had Macmillan wished to know them, which he didn't. The President was waiting. Butler cabled their agreement. The Prime Minister could act on his own terms. There obviously are *some* ways to get a quick—and favorable—decision out of HMG, especially if one is the Prime Minister who has a President to use as his excuse.

While Macmillan at Nassau was "waiting" for his colleagues, the Americans were thinking about France. How hard would this agreement hit our aims in Europe, never mind the PM's bland assurances? How was this form of "multilateral solution" to be fostered? How might we turn this deal to good account? De Gaulle stood at the center of all questions.

Answers for the moment seemed to lie in offering the French what we agreed to give the British. De Gaulle had shown no inclination to accept assistance for *his* nuclear force if there were any hint that aid might compromise its independence. But Britain's escape-clause might do for him as well as for Macmillan. An offer of POLARIS on the same terms might conceivably entice him back to NATO, to cooperation, even "integration." At the least it might induce him to be courteous at Brussels while he thought the matter over. (We did not know what he had said at Rambouillet, but knew enough of what the French were saying elsewhere to be nervous.) And at most, if he should spurn the offer, everyone would know that we had tried to deal with France just as we dealt with Britain. Therefore we should make him the same offer, and at once.

How to make de Gaulle an offer? Thought was given hurriedly to a dramatic gesture: Macmillan should fly back to France or Kennedy might go there. But neither picked the notion up and it got lost amidst distractions of last-minute work on the Communiqué. A letter then would be the vehicle. Bohlen had been brought to Nassau; *he* could go to Paris and pursue the matter orally. The letter could be short and he explanatory. So it was decided.

It also was decided to send Adenauer notice of what we had done for Britain and would now propose to France. His letter was dispatched and then delivered with such promptness that we could not call it back. But meanwhile we had realized that we did not know what it would take to deal with France and Britain even-handedly.

To offer France the "same" terms on POLARIS was insulting. Britain had the nuclear technology to build warheads and submarines; the French did not. How far they were from this we scarcely knew. We offered Britain missiles; to give France no more was to give less. But giving an equivalent meant moving toward direct support for French nuclear programs. We had avoided this before and in the process had lost touch with their programming. Even if we dropped our "no aid" policy, nobody knew at Nassau what the aid would have to be.

Therefore, pending study, "same" was changed to "similar" in the letter for de Gaulle. It proved too late to make that change in Adenauer's letter. No doubt the Elysée read both.

At Nassau the Americans monopolized concern about the French. Months later, the President reportedly told André Fontaine of *Le Monde* that our offer to de Gaulle had been suggested by Macmillan. If so it was a private hint which the PM did not think worth discussing with his people. No one on the British side, in London or in Paris, betrayed to me the least awareness that our offer had been anything but sheer "public relations." No one saw the least significance in substituting "similar" for "same." Macmillan *may* have planted the idea—Ball, Tyler, Nitze were also on the scene—but not, apparently, with any serious purpose. Where de Gaulle was concerned, the PM ceded *seriousness* to us. Five days had passed since Rambouillet and now he had POLARIS to bring home.

On Friday, December 21, the Nassau Conference ended. The President went off to Palm Beach, taking Gore and Bohlen with him. Bohlen flew to Paris shortly after. The PM's party lingered on for talks with the Canadians, then flew home in high spirits. It had been a hard week, but not a bad one.

Their elation was short-lived. Large sections of the British press and of the Tory party saw them coming without SKYBOLT and transporting home instead the paper promise of a costly, NATO-tied, American device which did not fit V-bombers and would go in vessels yet unbuilt. For that matter, the missiles were not built; the PM had insisted on A-3's. Initial press reaction was to cry "defeat." The House was happily in recess. Tempers were not improved by an announcement from our Air Force of what loosely was described as a successful test for SKYBOLT. This was almost the last gasp of Air Force resistance, but the British did not know that until later.

Meanwhile, the rest of the Americans flew back to Washington and went to see the Secretary of State.

XIII. "Post-Nassau Planning"

The Americans who flew to Washington from Nassau were relaxed in relief at the conclusion of a difficult, potentially disruptive confrontation. In their relief they all were optimistic for the future. But their mutual confidence had diverse sources. Each man looked to the future from his own predisposition; each saw in Nassau's outcome opportunities to further the particular perspective with which he himself viewed "basic NATO policy" and European prospects.

McNamara and Nitze were particularly pleased. The POLARIS offer to the British, with its NATO assignment *and* escape-clause, seemed to them a perfect formula on which negotiation with the French could be begun. "If 'Skybolt' hadn't happened, it should have been invented. . . ." The negative decision of six months before could now be set aside. De Gaulle, like Macmillan, might find this formula sufficiently protective for the independence of his national deterrent. If so, the French could "rejoin" NATO with their *force de frappe* for targeting and planning. This might not be ideal but would be an improvement, as close as one could come, in present circumstances, toward "integration" of French nuclear forces. Once negotiation began, on this formula, de Gaulle might be enticed by warheads and by submarines. Thus "similar" could be rendered "equivalent."

Nitze visualized another "spoke" in his "wheel"; McNamara visualized French funds for conventional forces. And if negotiation proved that de Gaulle was *not* interested, even on the basis of this formula, we would know where we stood with him once and for all. Even a negative outcome could improve the *status quo*: it would put to rest all doubt about our prior negativism.

In the perspective of these two men from Defense, "multilateral" meant "multinational" for us, for Britain, and for France, but it could *also* mean "Smith-Lee" for Germans and for lesser fry, as one component of a NATO nuclear force, tied to NATO targeting and tied to us through our participation—still another spoke for Nitze's wheel.

Ball saw all this differently. The British formula was worth supporting if it made life bearable for Tories while they did their work of bringing Britain into EEC. It was worth offering the French since a negotiation might entangle them in such a way as to assure complaisance toward the British at the coming round of talks on EEC. But once the British had got into "Europe," we should modify that formula as fast as possible, and work our way back to the safe ground of a "truly" multilateral solution—MLF. Otherwise, the German problem would remain to haunt us. So long as France and Britain were enabled with our aid to maintain something different and more national, "Smith-Lee" was bound to imply a "discrimination" against Germans. When we could, we should return to our attack on national forces. MLF remained the route. And meanwhile we should reassure the Germans that it remained our goal for everybody, not just them.

Like his colleagues from Defense, the Undersecretary of State was pleased at Nassau's outcome, but what pleased him most was the term "multilateral," so used as to retain a connotation of "mixed-manned." From this Ball drew some personal satisfaction; he recalls, "If the Secretary had gone and I'd stayed home, MLF would have been lost entirely."

As for Bundy, it was later said in State that he had liked the outcome "because he saw something in it for everybody, a typical 'Dean's solution.'" If so, his liking seems entirely reasonable in light of *his* responsibilities as aide to the one man who needed most to know how forces were arrayed, where history was tending, before he put his own foot down irrevocably. Indeed, what seems less reasonable is that as the weeks passed Bundy, among others, was unable to control the bureaucratic process by which balances were upset faster than the White House wanted and an outsize "Merchant Mission," more bludgeon than scalpel, turned a probe of MLF into "commitment." But that is another story.

When their plane touched down in Washington, these five drove to the State Department and saw Rusk. They reported on the recent past and canvassed future prospects. It was generally agreed that there would have to be intensive follow-up on all aspects of Nassau: a sales-agreement for the British, an examination of the bases for negotiation with the French, a look into the ways and means for NATO nuclear forces, both "multinational" and "truly" multilateral, including adaptation of the Smith-Lee offer. It also was agreed that State should lead the follow-up, assembling inter-agency task forces for the purpose. Rusk prepared to get this under way at once. Taking him aside, McNamara urged that it be put in other hands than Owen's or Schaetzel's. Rusk thereupon named Kitchen as his representative to lead the total effort and to chair a "steering group" with sub-groups for each phase. In the next days Kitchen was to draw on men from both Departments. As he did so, Owen was assigned to the sub-group on MLF and Schaetzel to the sub-group on France. This may not have been quite what McNamara intended, but subordinate assignments were "details" and the authority was Rusk's. Both at the start and later, the Secretary of Defense forebore to press the point beyond Kitchen's level.

Once the general outline of "next steps" had been agreed, McNamara and Nitze flew west for the holidays. Ball and Bundy went their ways. Rusk started Kitchen off and set December 28 for an initial meeting with his group. Then Christmas intervened.

Had there been any opportunity to influence the French, that intervention, although brief, seems fatal.

The President was in Palm Beach for Christmas. On his way there from Nassau, he and Bohlen had discussed our offer to the French. Bohlen recalls:

> The President was in no sense optimistic about the prospects of negotiation with the French. At no point in our conversation did he suggest that he was ready to give warhead or submarine assistance to the

French. But I got the clear impression that he had not excluded these possibilities. What he wanted above all was to get the General into serious negotiation and establish some real contact. He knew that if we started, and if de Gaulle were forthcoming, warheads and submarines might follow. He wasn't excluding them as possibilities. On the other hand, he had very much in mind the Congressional hazards, and other hazards, if he were to go that far and when we talked he wasn't ready to assume he'd have to. He knew we wouldn't have to if de Gaulle acted as usual. But this is not to say he was unwilling to. . . .

In some such frame of mind, the President received the French Ambassador, Hervé Alphand, just after Christmas. The White House files do not disclose the date, but Gore who was a house guest recalls that Alphand afterwards,

. . . came out like a "cock-of-the-walk." He intimated plainly that the President had given him a hint which made him happy. He could smell warheads at the end of the road. Maybe *our* warheads, which would have been all right. If they got into a serious negotiation he could see that at the end "similar" would be converted into "equal," perhaps in a tri-partite context.

But Alphand evidently did not convey this impression to his government. Or if he did the French chose to dilute it. An American correspondent was informed by French officials that Alphand found Kennedy "non-committal" about warheads.

If that was the Alphand report, he may have had some reason to temper his initial show of optimism. On instruction from the Elysée, reportedly, the French were out in force for ten days after Nassau, attempting to gauge Washington's intentions. On December 27, their Counselor of Embassy quizzed Schaetzel on the matter. Schaetzel's notes record:

He asked what a "similar arrangement with France" meant. I said we were still developing our thinking . . . but my personal view was that it ought to be considered exactly similar to the arrangements worked out with the British. . . . I said it presumably excluded technical warhead assistance and presumably the British and the French would construct their own nuclear submarines. . . .

Schaetzel was in for a surprise. The next day he joined other members of the Kitchen group to hear his Secretary lay down lines for them to follow. With respect to French negotiations, Schaetzel's special charge, the minutes of that meeting show:

> . . . Mr. Schaetzel . . . did not think we could or should at this time at-tempt to have [Bohlen], in his initial discussions with the French, am-plify on the Nassau Agreement. The Secretary agreed this would be premature since the details were yet to be developed. However, he stated that the discussions should . . . avoid a premature foreclosure to a full exchange of views. . . .
>
> The Secretary stated . . . that all alternatives should be explored at this time. . . . While he did not, for example, believe we should indi-cate our immediate willingness to provide nuclear assistance to France, even this previous fundamental policy should be re-evaluated in light of Nassau. The key would be a sufficiently fundamental change in French policy. The immediate matter, however, was not to judge . . . but rather to explore all possible avenues. . . .

Without enthusiasm, Schaetzel did as he was told. He organized his sub-group and called two meetings which were marked by clashes be-tween members from Defense and State with different views of "ur-gency" and differing degrees of ignorance about French nuclear pro-grams. The group then turned to study without meeting. They still were doing so on January 14.

Meanwhile, after some debate in Schaetzel's group and elsewhere, State cabled Bohlen, now back at his post. The cable contained his "in-structions." These reached him January 2. He was not very pleased to have them after Nassau and Palm Beach:

> . . . the points that should be given particular emphasis are first, that the U.S. is prepared to make a major decision of policy and to accord to France—at least so far as the Nassau proposals are concerned— the same status as Britain, but only on the understanding that the French themselves revise their policy to accept the multilateral principle.
>
> . . . the French cannot at this juncture be apprised of the exact na-ture of further U.S. assistance, beyond the offer of the "similar ar-rangement," as suggested by the President in his letter to de Gaulle.

The American Ambassador proceeded to the Elysée and put his best foot forward with the President of the Republic. De Gaulle did not ap-pear enthused but Bohlen thought him interested and cheerfully "exceeded" State's instructions (as he read them). He did *not* exceed White House intent. De Gaulle was told, in Bohlen's recollection, that "no possibilities were excluded, all relationships were open for discussion"; our offer from Nassau represented "a beginning, not an end." The end would be discovered through negotiation. We were eager for a serious exploration. But we lacked the information to proceed alone; we hoped the French would join us.

Bohlen left the Elysée quite hopeful of the outcome. De Gaulle, he thought, would probably negotiate to see what did lie at the end and at what price. Bohlen was aware that if the General did so he could not, at the same time, be beastly to the British. And our man's hopes were raised by what his English colleague told him. The British Ambassador also saw the General; de Gaulle had volunteered that he intended to be "cautious" in his forthcoming press conference, January 14. This cheered the Englishman, and Bohlen too.

In Washington, meanwhile, Owen had produced a memorandum analyzing Nassau's impact on our European policy. He wrote:

> 1. *Problem.* Nassau left us with two tracks to pursue:
> (a) Missile help for UK and French national MRBM forces, in return for these countries' commitments to support and eventually include their Polaris forces in a multilateral force.
> (b) Creation of a multilateral mixed manned force, which would be open to all NATO nations.
>
> 2. *Basic Course.* It is in our interest to press ahead vigorously with the second track.
> This will tend to absorb German and Italian post-Nassau nuclear pressures. . . . Moreover, progress toward a multilateral force will betoken to these countries the possible eventual end of UK and French national Polaris forces and thus the possible end of intra-European discrimination. . . .

On those premises he urged that NATO organs and the Germans should be reassured of our fidelity to pre-existing policy pronouncements, and should have authoritative word that MLF remained our favored "track."

The logic appealed widely inside State, and elsewhere there was general recognition of a need for soothing noises at the Porte Dauphine and Bonn. Even in Defense, where Owen's premises were scarcely shared, there was no disposition to *ignore* the Germans. Ball met no opposition when he volunteered to explain Nassau to them.

On January 10, the Undersecretary flew to Paris for a session with the North Atlantic Council. While there he spent some time with the French Foreign Minister, Couve de Murville. Ball passed a pleasant evening with his English colleague Heath, who also had seen Couve and had been told that if the British came to terms on technical issues "no power on earth" could keep them out of EEC. Ball then flew to Bonn, and on the morning of the 14th met with Adenauer. As Ball recalls, that meeting fully justified his trip:

> . . . The Chancellor began by saying "This morning I awoke with the terrible feeling that this was the day I would have a serious dis-agreement with the Americans." Before the morning ended he was reassured. When I started to describe what we had in mind by Paragraph 7 of the Nassau Communiqué, Adenauer asked "Is this the Smith-Lee force?" When I said "Yes" he brightened visibly and expressed satisfaction.

To our Ambassador in Paris, *nothing* justified Ball's trip. No matter how pleased he had made the Chancellor that morning, Bohlen blames him for what de Gaulle did that afternoon:

> When George saw Couve he told him that the whole emphasis of Nassau's multilateral arrangements was on the mixed-manned force. Couve expressed surprise. Clearly, if this is what Nassau did mean, de Gaulle could have no conceivable interest in it. No doubt he heard of it from Couve and then attached George's words to everything I had told him. . . .
>
> Until then I think he had seen the "multilateral" business as some-thing for the somewhat distant future. Meanwhile, with our help he could speed up creation of his national forces. Then, when the future came to be decided he would have an equal voice in working out what "multilateral" should mean, if anything, beyond NATO assignment.
>
> Now George had changed the *timing*. George made it sound as though what we were after was a quick move toward very tight, essentially non-national arrangements. If this was our timing the whole thing be-came plainly unacceptable. That's what surprised Couve. I think it's what decided de Gaulle.

This is interesting but rather hard to credit; de Gaulle, reportedly, commits to memory every line he utters in "press conference." Bohlen's view presumes a heavy task of memorization in one week-end.

Couve reportedly discounts this view on more substantial grounds. He recently told Brandon, among others, that his master's sense of Nassau had been much like that in most initial English press reports: Macmillan forfeited "independence," lost his fight, came home without the national deterrent he had told the French at Rambouillet he would maintain. This is alleged as the decisive factor in de Gaulle's response to Nassau, a factor present before Ball arrived upon the scene.

British Foreign Office sources disbelieve both explanations. In their eyes the "decisive factor" antedated Rambouillet. The General had decided that they should not enter EEC. If so, he had to turn our nuclear offer down, or else risk their ability to bargain their way in. Nassau gave him a dramatic chance to slam the door, no "ifs," or "buts," or technical obscurities. Why should de Gaulle the dramatist deny himself this chance to do what he would otherwise have done by other means? There was nothing to dissuade him but our uncertain "beginning." We could not offer more; that could not be enough. We missed no "opportunity"; there was none to be taken.

In the British Defence Ministry, the retrospect is different. Thorneycroft himself remarks:

> You never could and never will get de Gaulle into nuclear collaboration with *you*. It is too transatlantic. He means it when he says he will not let France "down." It is we who can bring him into collaboration, with us and so with you. Our joint deterrent could be linked with yours through NATO. That is the only way. But just as he can't be a "demandeur" with us, so we can't be with you. . . .
>
> You must tell us we can carry our technology across the Channel. We can't ask. To do so would cast doubt upon us. You might want to stop sharing secrets with us from then on. Very well. But you must free us to share past secrets with them. . . .

This is quite a statement from a Minister familiar with Macmillan, a man who did not hesitate in 1957 to "ask" us to amend the Atomic Energy Act, and at Camp David three years later asked for SKYBOLT. To Thorneycroft, I take it, this is a debater's point (and I a member of the House).

He continues:

> We wouldn't propose that course to you before Nassau. But in my personal opinion if *you* had proposed it we'd be in the Common Market

now and France would be in the Alliance, with us and with you. . . .
My colleagues didn't think we could "buy our way in" [to EEC]. I
don't agree.

This is the course we shall all have to take some day. We could have
done it in 1962.

So the Foreign Office and Defence contend. Their views of past events
are not without significance today, witness the Cabinet on MLF. Regardless, one or another may be right, and Bohlen wrong, and Couve a
rationalizer. Nobody *knows* except de Gaulle.

On January 14, the General staged his drama. When he met the press
that afternoon he let them know that he would keep the British out of
Europe. Much of what Macmillan had been told a month before was
now put on the public record:

> England is, in effect, insular, maritime, linked through its trade, mar-
> kets and food supply to very diverse and often very distant coun-
> tries. . . . In short, the nature, structure and economic context of En-
> gland differ profoundly from those of the other States of the Continent.
>
> One was sometimes led to believe that our English friends, in apply-
> ing for membership in the Common Market, agreed to change their
> own ways even to the point of applying all the conditions accepted
> and practiced by the Six, but, the question is to know if Great Britain
> can at present place itself, with the Continent. . . .
>
> One cannot say that it has now been resolved. Will it be so one
> day? Obviously Britain alone can answer that. . . .
>
> . . . It is possible that Britain would one day come round to trans-
> forming itself enough to belong to the European Community without
> restriction and without reservation, and placing it ahead of anything
> else, and in that case the Six would open the door to it and France
> would place no obstacle in its path. . . .
>
> It is also possible that England is not yet prepared to do this, and
> that indeed appears to be the outcome of the long, long Brussels
> talks. . . .

The General then proceeded to reject our Nassau offer:

> France has taken note of the Anglo-American Nassau agreement. As
> it was conceived, undoubtedly no one will be surprised that we cannot
> subscribe to it. It truly would not be useful for us to buy Polaris mis-
> siles when we have neither the submarines to launch them nor the
> thermonuclear warheads to arm them. . . . In other words, for us, in
> terms of technology, this affair is not the question of the moment.

But also, it does not meet with the principle . . . which consists of
disposing in our own right of our deterrent force. To turn over our
weapons to a multilateral force, under a foreign command, would be
to act contrary to that principle of our defense and our policy. It is
true that we too can theoretically retain the ability to take back in our
hands, in the supreme hypothesis, our atomic weapons incorporated
in the multilateral force. But how could we do it in practice during the
unheard of moments of the atomic apocalypse? And then, this multilateral force necessarily entails a web of liaisons, transmissions and in-
terferences within itself, and on the outside a ring of obligations such
that, if an integral part were suddenly snatched from it, there would
be a strong risk of paralyzing it just at the moment, perhaps, when it
should act.

In sum, we will adhere to the decision we have made: to construct
and, if necessary, to employ our atomic force ourselves.

Quite unmistakably, the General understood and *did not like* precisely what attracted McNamara and Nitze: an approach toward integration, a transatlantic tie, a "web of liaisons, transmissions, and inter-
ferences." De Gaulle cared *more* for independence than Macmillan. His
concern went beyond symbols (or "beginnings") to specifics. De Gaulle,
in French, was talking McNamara's language as he turned his back on
McNamara's aims.

In Brussels, two weeks later, the French halted Britain's effort to join
EEC. The Six could not continue to negotiate. Heath went home.

In London, the PM prepared to face —and to face down—an outcry
from his parliamentary critics. History now helped him: he could speak
of the Americans as friends and France spoke for herself. Many Tories
were relieved; next to getting into EEC triumphantly, there was no better posture than to be kept out by *Frenchmen*. Macmillan may have
sensed this all along. Disinterest in our offer to the French suggests
he did.

At any rate, the PM got through House debate without losing his
hold upon POLARIS. For this de Gaulle deserves some credit, also Kennedy. As one of Thorneycroft's assistants put it: "That television program in December really helped us with the RAF and Navy and their
friends. If they wanted a deterrent force at all, and links to you, they
had to climb aboard POLARIS after that."

In Washington, amidst the ruin of assorted hopes for other things,
the budget went to Congress without SKYBOLT. The President's TV remarks a month before were amplified in telling fashion, and the cancel-

lation now appeared in context of the deficit. This "last act" of my story evoked minimal reaction. The Air Force scarcely raised its head and friends in Congress scarcely bothered to complain. For many Washingtonians "Skybolt" remains a dirty word. Hitch is not among them.

While the budgetary issue vanished from the scene, officials alternately cursed de Gaulle and canvassed their constricted range of choice. The Merchant Mission followed in due course.

XIV. Conclusion

An appraisal of this story is a matter for judgment. In what follows I have drawn upon my own. Every point is arguable. Readers are on notice.

To appraise the story one must first decide what were its costs and benefits for whom. If evidence sustained the charge that it "caused" de Gaulle's check to Monnet's Europe, it might well deserve the label of "disaster" which was often pasted on it after January 14. I find nothing to sustain the charge. The outcome, then, was no disaster for our Government. But this is not to say it cost us nothing.

What were the costs to us?

First, we gave de Gaulle a stage-set for his drama; he is ingenious and he might have done as well without, but we made easy what might have come hard. Second, when his action blighted many other hopes, the MLF emerged as something we could cling to; we clung and got committed in the process with no company of note except the Germans. Whether this will turn out to have been a long-term benefit, nobody knows. In the short run I include it as a cost because it is so plainly what the constitutional conductor of our foreign relations did *not* want.

Third, we paved the way toward this result, and others, by intensifying paranoid reactions in our own officialdom. After Nassau, Indians were more estranged from Chiefs than they had been before, and more discordant in relations with each other. Three indicative examples: Kitchen and Schaetzel, for a time, stopped speaking to each other. Owen and Rowen more or less lost touch. Rostow still thinks Nassau a disaster. Another indication: Schaetzel and Owen, among others, see the Secretary of Defense as an inveterate meddler in their Secretary's business. McNamara sees them as Rusk's Admiral Andersons. Paranoid reactions are not quite confined to Indians.

Fourth, we deposited on top of Suez new stuff to feed paranoid reactions in Great Britain. Transatlantic attitudes resemble trans-Potomac ones. Not merely Tory right-wingers but many correspondents of "respectable" papers, some officials in major Ministries, some Ministers, some would-be Ministers, are a degree more wary of us after SKYBOLT than before. Last summer's brief eruption of Establishment suspiciousness about the *Newsweek* piece on their security is traceable directly to the wounds of eight months earlier. In July 1963, reportedly, it was alleged by "informed" civil servants, never mind the press, that Kennedy himself had planted the piece as an excuse for scuttling our Agreement on POLARIS.

The Thorneycrofts of Britain—who are not confined to Tory ranks— regard their ties to us as matters of *cold* interest, and are more inclined than ever to believe we do the same. The senior civil servants who regarded us most warmly after war-collaboration are retired, or retiring, in droves. Suspicion spreads with fewer checks than formerly, and SKY- BOLT helped to spread it.

Fifth, in many circles on the Continent, this Skybolt-Nassau sequence fed the sense that our conceptions and our execution were alike erratic. More importantly, it left a base on which later impressions could pile up, not least in the ensuing course of MLF and dollar-saving exercises. In short, we drew down our political credit.

Sixth, to some degree we did the same at home, and left a sense of disarray, improvisation, "trouble," casting doubt upon the credit-line extended after Cuba. This story seems the least of causes for such doubts among our wider public, but within our own bipartisan Establishment we surely paid some price, and still are paying.

Seventh, and most speculative, we "lost" what *maybe* was a chance to further our proclaimed concern for European unity and strategic integration. Nassau *may* have been an opportunity; McNamara *may* have been correct in thinking "Skybolt" was an issue worth inventing to produce that opportunity. *If* the President and PM had been able to keep their minds on de Gaulle; *if* he had been, or could have been induced to turn, a shade less French; *if* we had spent the months preceding Nassau thinking through a European nuclear deterrent based on Anglo-French collaboration; and *if* we had liked it when we thought it through—then Nassau would have set a different stage and Thorneycroft's prediction might have come to pass.

Were governing as easy as some journalists suppose, this "lost chance" should rank first among my costs. But there are far too many "ifs" in it for me. I note it but I'm not inclined to count it.

So much for costs to us, what of the benefits? First, we disencumbered our prospective defense budgets of $2.5 billion without fuss or fight in Congress; this is no mean feat. Second, we sustained Rusk's formula: "I'm not against the 'special relationship' until I can see something better to take its place." Thereby we kept "somebody to talk to." Also we averted far worse noises from our own Establishment than we have heard. A public breach with Britain would not have come cheap at home. Besides, it might have cost us dear abroad. We helped Macmillan squelch temptations toward Tory Gaullism. But more than this, we kept chips in our hands for later bargaining with Harold Wilson, the likely next Prime Minister, should *he* ever be tempted toward *Socialist* Gaullism. This seems to me decidedly a benefit for us.

Most Americans believe that such temptations have no substance, that whatever Tories—or the Labourites—might threaten, neither could bring off a British turn to anti-American continentalism. But Britain now is going through a phase of doubt, uncertainty, over the shape and meaning "of it all," a mood not wholly different from what we are always hearing of West Germans. Confidence about the "certitudes" of politics and policy may not be much more warranted in one case than the other. If so, Nassau was prudent and prudence a benefit.

To underscore the point it is worth noting that a year ago, during the Cuban crisis (until the worst was over), Oxford Dons who pride themselves on "knowing America" ascribed our stand to pre-election politics. It also is worth noting that in July Wilson told me:

> You Americans should understand that your support of Macmillan's deterrent will make me take an anti-German line. He is using the deterrent to play upon a widely-diffused patriotic sentiment among men in the pubs. I don't think this is as important as he does. I think the election will turn on domestic issues. But it isn't *un*important and I can't ignore it. So I shall have to play upon another widely-diffused sentiment, the only one available: anti-Germanism. I shall have to say that we must give up our deterrent to keep the bloody Germans from getting theirs. One counters emotion with emotion. I rather think the PM has the better line but I must take what is available. I know that Washington won't like it but I hope your people understand that they've left me no choice.

If the PM had got the "better line," might not Wilson once in office wish to take it for his own, reducing outcries from the left by giving it an "anti-capitalist" twist? Why would he not at least toy with this tactic? One need neither dislike him nor "suspect" him to regard it as a tactic worth consideration in his terms—especially if he should find some continental Socialist regimes with which to make, or at least claim, a common cause. The Anglo-American relationship, sustained at Nassau, then would be a tie on him and good for us. Of this more later.

Taking costs and benefits together, I consider that our balance-sheet looks reasonably good. Once Skybolt was a crisis between Washington and London, hindsight fails to show me how we could have done much better in the flap which then prevailed. This raises a next question: need it have become a "crisis"? Before I turn to that, however, one more note on benefits and costs: in his own terms, whatever we may think of them, Macmillan's balance-sheet looks better than ours.

Strategically, the Tories had at stake last fall the future of their country, to say nothing of their party's hold on office. The stakes remain, and rise perhaps, since January 14. So we tend to see it. But tactically, for Tories, the next best thing to joining EEC "on decent terms" was an outright rejection by de Gaulle. The next best thing to SKYBOLT was POLARIS. So, at least, Macmillan evidently saw it. In the event he got his second-best. Silence in November and a crisis in December *helped* him do it. Given de Gaulle's stand at Rambouillet, Macmillan was in poor shape to achieve "first-best" on Europe; without Nassau he might well have had to settle for "third-best," a dragged-out death at Brussels which could seem his fault. And given our own budgeting, he was in *no* shape to achieve "first-best" on his deterrent. Under these conditions and in this imperfect world, to have achieved his "second-best" on both scores is not bad.

The PM did not "plan it that way," to be sure. But none of his own actions interfered with the result, and most of them contributed toward it, even that long silence which annoys some of us still. On that he followed our example.

From our standpoint as strategists Macmillan's conduct may not measure up to "his" strategic stakes, by which we usually mean our own attributed to him. From his standpoint the attribution probably is faulty. How many British politicians ever warmed to "strategy"? How many men in English life think such a thing worth having? Not many, I suspect, not anyway outside a few rooms in and near the Foreign Office and perhaps a few odd corners of the House. Macmillan, I assume, did not frequent such places. "Strategy" for him was evidently tantamount to general long-run hunches plus specific short-run tactics. In terms of tactics, second-best looks good.

From a Tory point of view, the look might be still better if their PM had claimed publicly that Nassau was a triumph of diplomacy, for "independence," *at our expense*. But noises on that subject loud enough to be convincing would have seriously embarrassed *us*. Macmillan too paid something to sustain Anglo-American relations, not least sitting on Thorneycroft but also keeping off the theme that he "outwitted" Kennedy.

Unless Sir Alec Douglas-Home can pull a Truman on the pollsters, a key issue for us in the next months of those relations becomes *how to fashion institutionalized substitutes* for the cantankerous but sturdy pro-Americanism of Macmillan. Or so it seems to me. Of this also, more later.

Now for that next question. Did there have to be a "crisis"? Almost certainly there had to be some fuss. Macmillan's tactical dexterity brought him to seek and buy a pig-in-a-poke at Camp David. McNamara's vigorous pursuit of cost-effectiveness was bound, in time, to put us back on the collision course his predecessor charted merely months after Camp David. The PM made what seems to me a classic error in high policy or politics: he pursued objectives, diplomatic and political, disguised as something else, a military posture, which was unconvincing on its face, in its own terms, *and* hard to hold. We cannot be too critical of him; from 1960 into 1963 we did the same with MLF. But this for us was not a dearest object, or not then, while his deterrent always had that quality for him. Once *he* tied it to *our* pursuit of SKYBOLT, he embedded trouble in our mutual relations.

Trouble was rendered the more likely by our change of Administration, which removed the men who had dealt with Macmillan at Camp David. It was rendered still more so by their deal's survival through one budget season under each Administration. The third budget season coincided with a fall in Tory fortunes and a turning-point at Brussels. Clearly, if we cancelled there was bound to be at least a private fuss.

But need a private fuss have turned into a public crisis? The answer probably is "no." Throughout November 1962, before the press got into the act, there were successive turning points at any one of which a different course of conduct on somebody's part might have forestalled that escalation. Like all such instances this study can be summarized, "for want of a nail, a shoe was lost, for want of a shoe. . . ." and so forth. Readers will have noted many moments when each actor might have done a little differently with large results.

Loose nails abound: At the White House, for example, had the President preceded McNamara on the transatlantic telephone November 9; or had Bundy put his own mind and the President's to work on what Hawthorne was trying to convey; or had the President conveyed with emphasis to others the procedural assurance he gave Gore before Thanksgiving; or had he and Gore got down to cases with each other then. At departmental levels had Kohler gone to Moscow three months later than he did; or had Rusk supplemented McNamara's word to Bruce; or had Rusk called for better staff work on November 24; or had McNamara been less busy after that; or had he shouldered what he knew to be his burden, surfacing his difference of opinion with Rusk's staff. At both levels had Cuba not occurred just when it did; or in its aftermath had McNamara's "I'll take care of it" carried a little less conviction to his auditors.

"Missed opportunities" like these, small matters-of-the-moment, litter the ground on our side and on London's side are others. In November the British missed fewer than we did; they used their quota but had fewer to miss. The initiative was ours.

Some of these nails may not come loose "next time." Experience conveys its own correctives. Bundy and de Zulueta, for example, know each other better than they did a year ago. From them and from their principals the private phone has had a lot of use since last November. As a second example, McNamara and Thorneycroft are not in the least likely to take one another for granted again.

But might-have-dones are not confined to momentary lapses at high levels. At lower levels one finds more enduring problems. It is by no means certain that experience has yet corrected these, or can.

One of the most revealing things in this entire story—indicative of a deep-seated problem—is the State Department letter of "instruction" to Defense, the three-alternatives letter of November 24. For what this indicates is that at upper official levels, where staff work was confined, State's Indians who took the lead in drafting neither grasped the "British problem," nor took time for thought about it, nor faced up to the dilemma it created for their Chiefs: how Washington's objectives could be *squared* with London's wants. By hindsight it is evident that they missed an extraordinary opportunity, had missed it for the three preceding weeks, would miss it for the three weeks after that, and have not seen it yet: the 50-50 offer. Had no one ever seen it I could not say that they "missed" it, but McNamara and Rusk in turn came close, and then the President at last produced it for himself.

The virtue of the 50-50 offer was *not* that had it been made earlier the British might have bought it; in terms of Hitch's tactics this could well be judged a vice. Nor was its virtue that a timely offer might have brought the Cabinet to dispense with their deterrent, thus delighting every Indian in sight. Despite the Blighs and Carys I am hard put to believe Macmillan would have wanted what we dropped, on any terms. I am even harder put to think that he could have been cornered by his Cabinet and deprived of his deterrent altogether.

What I find entirely easy to believe is that if we had made the 50-50 offer in November, Macmillan would have been at Nassau hat in hand, thanking the President for generosity and asking could he please have something else. It then should have been no trick to arrange joint-study while we both watched Brussels. If de Gaulle had proved adamant on EEC, we could have given London the POLARIS at less cost. If he had not, and Brussels were succeeding, London could have asked him to join their side of the study. One thinks of many variations on this theme, all likelier to meet *our* problem than the three "ungenerous" options of November 24.

The virtue of the 50-50 offer was precisely what the President saw in it and Gore used it for with half-success: a show of generosity so plain as to preclude anti-Americanism while putting off POLARIS. Even in December that virtue served us well, witness the effect on Thorneycroft. In November it should have sufficed to spare us from or mute a public crisis.

But in fact it took the crisis to secure White House attention; it took Kennedy himself to see the needed virtues and to find them in this offer at the tag-end of the day. Where were the Indians meanwhile? They were intent on Europe and on non-proliferation, comforting themselves with Bowie's happy thought that they could use the President as though he were a bludgeon to be wielded in support of *their* priorities. They scarcely gave a thought to his priorities and still cannot conceive that theirs and his could be *legitimately* different.

Superficially, the finger points to personalities. Since last November, frequent repetition of the same sort of behavior has aroused harsh comment about European-oriented Indians in general and two in particular: Schaetzel and Owen.

These two have certain natural advantages in drawing such attention to themselves. Both are determined, dedicated public servants, with a vigorous concern for public causes which the White House much admired when the Kennedy Administration first came on the scene. They share a distinction among State Department officers in higher ranks: they have managed to survive and rise for many years without accepting the restraints of "Wristonization." They share other distinctions also. Both men are articulate beyond the capabilities of most associates. Both have enjoyed—and still parade—connections in "high places," a matter still significant to many of their colleagues: Schaetzel with Ball, Owen with Bundy. Bundy still is hard put to resist the lure of Owen's interesting mind, clean prose, and indefatigable staff work. Hardly anyone can. Ball's coincidence of purpose keeps his door open to Schaetzel. Rostow, Owen's nominal superior, has status as a family friend. Tyler, Schaetzel's nominal superior, has status as cheese in a sandwich.

But "personalities" cannot suffice as explanation for enduring problems; at any rate these personalities cannot. Gripes against "bureaucrats" now rain upon their heads. In the course of my interviewing, I have heard with frequency that "answers" lie in cutting off their heads. I doubt it. The sources of those gripes run deeper than these men. Exile the two tomorrow and the problem now attributed to *them* will still remain. This is not to argue what their next assignments ought to be. That is Secretary Rusk's business, not mine. This is to argue against action on false premises.

Consider my example of State's letter last November when the Indians were actually these men. There are five things one can criticize in their performance: a blinkered view of policy, limited perceptivity, low tolerance for listening, unconcern for feed-back, and a tendency to shove. It may be that a Schaetzel and an Owen, men of passion and frustration, are predisposed toward these things. *But heredity was certainly encouraged by environment.* Look at each item on this list in turn:

First, these men brought to SKYBOLT as an issue, and to the consideration of alternatives, their own policy perspectives. They ranked objectives and assigned priorities by light of *their* official duties; *their* bureaucratic interests, *their* personal ideas. But so did everybody else, a Nitze and a Rowen quite as much as they, to say nothing of others in this story. And *everybody* had a warrant, or at least a hunting-license, signed by John F. Kennedy, to certify his own views as "Administration policy."

The "Policy Directive" of 1961 seems to be unique in this regime; one may count one's blessings and be thankful for that. But even if the "Green Book" had contained no ambiguities, there would have been enough of these in Presidential speeches between May 1961 and July 1962, let alone the addresses of others. There were also ambiguities in private, to judge from many memoranda of conversations.

Over issues so complex as those encompassed by our "basic NATO policy" and hopes for Europe, Presidents are bound to have divided minds, especially while history has not disclosed to them where it is going. But when some sort of Presidential label is affixed to several sides of most divisions, the proponents of them all are free to "hunt" as best they can. So they did in this instance and so they will in future. Policing is a White House job, not theirs. From the standpoint of the issuing authority, some licenses may be better than others. But why expect the licensees to read all that fine print? He who draws distinctions must enforce them (if he can). That is the law of *this* jungle.

Second, our two huntsmen, Schaetzel and Owen, did not perceive the manifold considerations, other than their own, which were to be decisive for their Chiefs. They did not read the fine print from the past, nor did they ponder what might lie ahead as it would look to those who had been writing fine. Mostly, these two men were satisfied to read what *they* had written. It misled them. But almost everyone, regardless of location, did something of the same sort in this story. If an Owen and a Schaetzel missed what mattered in Rusk's mind, a Rowen failed to fathom McNamara's. A little later Rostow failed to sense what was essential for the President. On occasion even Bundy, among the most perceptive actors on the stage, seems to have missed his cues in that regard.

Part of the reason for these non-perceptions is that Chiefs, in self-protection, tend to veil their thoughts. The fine print is put in invisible ink. This tendency seems strong, although not equal, in the Chiefs encountered here. The President may confuse other staffs but evidently not his own, not anyway when they take pains to probe his mind. From what I hear and read he is the best "de-briefer" of the three. His thoughts as well as actions seem available for reading by associates of Bundy's sort, if rather more at their option than his: what happened in the case of those assurances to Gore?

The Secretary of Defense appears somewhat less open even with his personal associates, to say nothing of others. This story shows him as a *selective* "de-briefer," who selectively turns off (or on) his confidences, witness Nitze, Rowen, Yarmolinsky in November and December.

As for the Secretary of State, he literally has no counterparts to Bundy or to McNamara's men, no personal associates whom he can call his own. And with the departmental officers who serve as substitutes, he evidently tends to do as on November 24 (and on September 8). He questions and he listens; only under provocation does he speak his mind. Apparently this is so rare that when it happens what he says may get the treatment his words got at Paris: in one ear and out the other, rationalized away.

Third, State's non-perceivers of what mattered to their Chiefs also were non-listeners for what mattered to others. These amount to the same tendency at work on different fronts. Who listened hard for hints from British sources? Who listened hard for hints from Pentagon sources? Who listened hard to dissidents inside the State Department? Not Schaetzel or Owen. They were influenced by Bowie who was saying what they wished to hear. They also listened long enough to Rowen and to Bundy to catch whatever reinforced their own perceptions. It seems that their ears were not closed, merely selective.

But throughout this story, listening in a selective fashion is typical of activists with operating jobs. McNamara's listening seems similarly selective, if rather more sophisticated. So does Ball's. By State Department standards, Schaetzel has an operating job. On paper Owen has a staff job, but he is so useful to so many operators that the term "staff" as applied to him draws a distinction without a difference. Both are activists, and both were "operating." They may have overdone their selectivity, but ears like theirs seem standard for the men who play such parts.

In this story's cast of characters the most sensitive ear apparently belongs to Tyler, ostensibly another operating officer who heard so well that in effect he ceased to operate. The most patient listener undoubtedly was Rusk. No doubt he found a gain in this; he also paid a price. The next best listeners—aside from a few scientists—were evidently Bundy and Rowen. The term "staff" has some meaning in their instances; they had the duty. As one task among many, they undertook to look-and-listen for their Chiefs. Unhappily, they did not look or listen long at corners.

The moral seems to be that listening and operating are distinctive tasks which do not fit together very well. No doubt there are *some* Renaissance Men equipped by temperament to do both things at once with equal skill. But I see nothing to suggest that there are many, not enough to staff the State Department. If so, it makes no sense to blame State's operators for not listening.

Fourth, these operators thought about our conduct toward Great Britain in entirely different terms than we would use—or at least tell ourselves to use—about a comparable act against the interests of a *hostile* country. There are, of course, real differences; Britain is our closest "friend." There *also* are some critical similarities. These seem to have gone almost unrecognized when State framed its alternative for SKY-

BOLT. But State was not alone in this. Owen and Schaetzel were two among many; Rowen with others was in their company; also Bundy, to say nothing of the President. Above the level of the British desk, which wrote in vain, the company included most of Washington.

Had Britain seemed more "enemy" than "friend" a likely question in November would have been: if we hurt them what harm can they do us? Had Britain been both hostile and powerful—a Russia—no doubt we then would have pursued that question carefully; the possibilities of harm become immense and obvious. But Britain being Britain nobody *pursued* that question, carefully or otherwise. And yet, in the event, the harm we felt might follow from a public breach with Britain quite sufficed to satisfy our Chiefs that they must do precisely what their Indians were trying to prevent. In November if the question had occasioned thought, this might have been foreseen.

By hindsight it is clear that what the framers of alternatives required in November was at once an understanding of reactions to our warning and a forecast of responses to the options we were framing: feed-back on the one and estimation of the other. The harm Britain might do to us depended on two things: how certain politicians would perceive what we had done, and how they then would calculate their means to counter us—in terms of *their own stakes* as *they* conceived them. Our chance to minimize the harm, or ward it off, depended on two more things: how we shaped their view of what we were about, and how we influenced the stakes they weighed in their own calculations. If we were in the habit of appraising friends as enemies, these things would have been in our minds as early as November. But we do not have that habit and such things were out-of-mind, for Owen and for Schaetzel and for all of their superiors.

All knew that we were pure in heart and meant no harm to Britain; we assumed our friends would know this because we did. Can one blame Indians for sharing the assumptions of their Chiefs? Especially while one complains of their insensitivity to what Chiefs think?

But even had subordinates attempted to pursue the question of what harm our friends might do us, it is far from clear that in November they—at Indian-level—could have got the information for an answer. The President might have learned something on the telephone, and so might Rusk or Bundy. Bruce might have learned something face-to-face. From Indian to Indian, however, from the State Department to our Foreign Service Officers in London, there was little they could learn. For the calculations of a Thorneycroft or a Macmillan include matters on which

FSOs are generally uninformed, unused to seeking information, poorly placed to get it: personal stakes, procedural stakes, bureaucratic and political stakes, as seen within the close confines of Whitehall.

If my experience is any guide, the keenest students of such matters are a handful of officials, mostly Treasury not Foreign Office, scattered through top reaches of their government. Who in our Embassy deals intimately with them? Our people there suffer three disadvantages: they won no "firsts" at Oxford or Cambridge or equivalent, they wear a "Foreign Office" label, and they have but little feeling for *our* "Treasury-types" or for *our* bureaucratic-politics as practiced outside State. A Bundy, I daresay, would soon learn every secret in the Cabinet Office and the Private Office; he looks so irresistibly like one of theirs to them. We have no Bundys at our Embassy in London. For that matter we have none on Tyler's staff in Washington. Nor have we any shuttling back and forth.

Had London been Moscow, the Kremlinologists would have come out in force during November. Where were our Whitehall-ologists? They scarcely exist.

Fifth and finally, our two Indians proved hard to "manage." In November they went after what they wanted with the drive and single-mindedness they later would display on MLF. Their immediate superiors were passive as this happened; Tyler kept his counsel, Rostow worked on other things. Indians with dissident opinions were outflanked or shoved aside. The Secretary of State, whose later conduct shows that he had mental reservations, saddled their blinkered horse for them and told his colleague at Defense to ride. The Secretary of Defense agreed to do it, fingers crossed. *Why?* Answers go beyond the operating style of Schaetzel or of Owen.

What this suggests is what these criticisms all suggest, that the main "missed opportunity" in this affair turns on two individuals whose conduct was conditioned by the operating styles of everybody else, emphatically including Tyler, Rostow, Ball, Rusk, McNamara, Bundy, and the President.

If this is a failure in management look to the managers, the Secretaries and the White House above all.

* * * * * * * * *

In the course of this story, especially its Nassau phase, the President attempted what he later tried with MLF, to trace a rather subtle line of ac-

tion through competing aspirations which were unresolved and unre-
solvable until time clarified unknowns. Such endeavors are impressive,
at least to me, and very Presidential. But from a bureaucratic point of
view they are almost unbearable; *the pain they cause is real.*

Our contemporary big bureaucracy is a blunt instrument, effectively
responsive to blunt challenges when gripped by a blunt policy. Its character was shaped in World War and in Cold War. To wield it on behalf
of subtlety against diffuse and contradictory challenges is an exceedingly
hard task of management. It is not rendered easier by the peculiar inter-
lock of operating styles suggested in this story.

Still, as we approach the fourth year of a first term I would not urge
busy men, with the responsibilities of governing and re-election on their
backs, to worry overmuch about their operating styles. Self-conscious-
ness may help, perhaps this story can induce it. But blame or *mea culpas*
would be silly. This was *not* a disaster, after all. Everybody's "vices" are
the obverse of his virtues; on the showing of this story virtues dominate.
"Management improvement" is no pearl to be discovered by restyling
all our topmost personnel. (Besides, how would one go about it?) The
same thing can be said of structure and procedure at their level. On the
showing of this story, none of these *requires* change and change would
work no miracles.

From "Skybolt" as an issue in our policy-making I draw a simple lesson: regardless of structures or procedures, much of what occurred here
will occur again. How much depends upon the vigilance (and luck) of
individuals, especially of those who have the duty to protect their Chiefs,
a Bundy at the White House and his counterparts elsewhere. Throughout this story most of what went wrong cast shadows in advance. There
was no lack of clues; the lack was time, or thought, to pick them up
and read them. Bundy, in particular, is an accomplished juggler of many
balls at once. He juggles while he skates, and skates so fast that even
in a close-up like this story he himself remains a blur—which is as it
should be with a staff officer. But sometimes one ball or another crunches
through the ice; recovery is costly. One wonders whether Bundy might
not need a Bundy of his own. Whether he could use one is another matter. I am inclined to doubt it; he also needs (and likes) to travel light.
However that may be, avoiding other "Skybolts" is a problem, day by
day, for men in Bundy's line of work. If there are no such men at State,
if at Defense they are turned on-and-off, the larger the problem for
Bundy.

"Management improvement" means more-of-the-same but better done. This problem will not yield to institution-building.

"Skybolt" as an issue in Anglo-American relations is on a different footing. My study does suggest a high priority for thought and work on institution-building *with the British*. Bilateral relationships are frowned on in some quarters lest they become "exclusive." I do not see why they should. If we now need institutionalized substitutes for Macmillan, the Germans still appear to need such substitutes for Dulles. We ought to work on both. While we are waiting for our own election, and for theirs, and for Paris, and for Rome to clarify the "Europe" we shall deal with in a second term, this sort of work appears to me decidedly worth doing.

Where might we put our thoughts? Not into over-arching mechanisms, shadow enterprises, or another set of staffs at NATO (a place with all the verve of our Department of Commerce). Already we have more than enough of these. Rather, I suggest, we ought to think about unpublicized joint ventures, government to government, which actually put bureaucrats to work on matters relevant for them *and for their Ministers* in the internal conduct of each government—and so affect the stakes a Ministry will weigh as it participates in shaping national policy.

Our money and our weaponry have ceased to be decisive; if we wish a steady influence upon "alliance policy," which is but a reflection of *national* decisions, we must get down to the boiler rooms where such decisions start. We need to help each fireman do what matters to *him*, until at last he cannot think of shovelling without us. Of course he will not think it if he has not been inside *our* boiler room and found it useful in *his* business to be there. I see no point in starting a "joint venture" which we are not ready to pursue in common at decision-making levels. Anything else is "joint" *à la* SKYBOLT, which was not joint at all and surely is a model *not* to follow.

Assuming we can contemplate some genuine joint ventures, two spheres suggest themselves for careful exploration: research-and-development and defense budgeting.

If a Labour Government takes office in Great Britain, the uniform impression I have gained from shadow-ministers is that they look to us for psychic satisfaction in the form of "consultation." They think of their inheritance, POLARIS, as their trading-stock. But I doubt that it can buy them what they want. What they talk of wanting seems to me a lot less satisfying in office than out: Ministers of State attendant on the President, staff officers attendant on the JCS, and so forth. These evidently mean more to a shadow-government than a real Government is likely to find in them. The more one knows about *our* crisis operations and "war plans," the less there is to dignify the shadow-concepts of those shadow-ministers.

Disillusion, I suspect, will follow the enlightenment obtainable in office. Before that time arrives it would be helpful if there were a wide variety of ventures under way between our governments, which civil servants knew to be, and Ministers would find to be, of *use* in their own work and also ours. Budgeting and "R-and-D" are a far cry from Great Decisions; this is to their advantage. Down in the depths of governmental processes where incremental choices year by year shape later options day by day, joint ventures offer something *real* to buttress "consultation." Ministers and their machines might gain a lot from this, and we as well: their stakes become our ties on their Prime Minister.

With Britain we have numerous connections even now, many of them relics of the War, some new, some in the talk-stage. These span more spheres than defense and include intelligence. In some spheres, notably defense, the talk of new departures both at Whitehall and the Pentagon is well advanced. But so far as I have found, on casual inquiry, present connections and proposed ones are *uneven*. Some may engage real interests, create stakes, for key officials in both governments. Most apparently do not. Many seem to wander in a vacuum, disconnected from decisions by the national establishments. Some are invisible at a first glance.

As a guide to institution-building with the British, it may be well to survey what is now in place or planned, and why it grew, and how it works, *to whose advantage* in both governments. A survey of that sort might show some fatal flaws in trying to make any such bureaucratized joint ventures serve the political purpose sketched above. If so, I would be sorry but inclined to try again. We then should look for *other* means to "institutionalize Macmillan." The need remains.

That need is the main lesson I draw from "Skybolt" as an issue in our foreign relations. By extension I would guess that it applies no less to institution-building with the Germans.

3

British Refinements

On July 30, 1963, Harold Macmillan, still Prime Minister, approved my "unofficial" request to interview his Private Secretaries, along with Peter Thorneycroft, still Defence Minister, and some others. The PM did so as a courtesy to President Kennedy, on the assurance that my report would be strictly for the latter, and would critique the Washington performance in dealing with London, not the British performance per se.

But Macmillan didn't like it much. Lord Home, the Foreign Secretary, and Thorneycroft, along with the Lord Privy Seal—Edward Heath, who knew me—had to coax him into it. They decided, as the internal record shows, that my interviewees "should not give Professor Neustadt any paper. . . ." To make sure, the PM scribbled in the margin of the Foreign Office memo before him, "I agree. But it is important not to have a document. Otherwise it will all be in Newsweek before you can say 'McNamara.'"[1]

So the British narrative in my report to President Kennedy was based solely on interviews (unlike the American, for which I also had access to everyone's files). However, British records are made public after thirty years. What do they show that differs from or enhances my report? That is the question for consideration in this chapter; first differences, then enhancements.

I

Macmillan's instruction no doubt explains why the only papers I was shown in London during August 1963—as I pursued my inquiry for JFK—were transcripts of transatlantic or cross-channel meetings, and then only certain pages, one at a time, and literally shown—held out across the desk so I could read, by craning, while the owner kept a hand-hold (or kindly read to me).

The PM's posture also suggests that a subtext in all my British interviews may have been the paucity of other sorts of paper. Without hypothesizing such a subtext, I am at a loss to explain, from a distance of thirty-five years, why I made such a point in my 1963 report of Thorneycroft's lack of written communication with the Foreign Secretary and the Prime Minister, once a minute on the phone call of November 9, 1962, to Robert McNamara had been passed along. There is nothing so explicit in the finished memoranda of conversation I drew from my rough notes of interviews. Why else was I unequivocal?

With respect to written communication in Whitehall, somebody or something led me astray.

This is one of the few errors of fact I find in my 1963 narrative of British behavior during 1962, now that it can be compared with relevant British governmental files, which are mostly open today.[2] They show the Defence Minister was quite meticulous in keeping the PM informed, both orally and in writing. There was nothing exceptionally reticent in their communication with each other or with Lord Home. Nor did they misunderstand each other during the long wait for McNamara to arrive. (In this, Macmillan's aide Timothy Bligh remembered better than his colleague Philip de Zulueta.)

For instance, on the eve of McNamara's visit, Thorneycroft wrote Macmillan outlining how he proposed to deal with the American. If the latter seemed open to argument, he would argue. But if McNamara brought definitive word that Skybolt indeed was canceled, the British minister would first seek an assurance of American support for the independence of Britain's deterrent (the PM's crown jewel, of course). If, but only if, he got that, he would go on to explore Polaris, sharing with the PM the Navy's present preferences along with a rough sketch of comparative costs. Otherwise he'd stonewall, which is precisely what he did: ". . . I cannot pursue. . . . I will report to you, and you will certainly wish to press the President."[3]

What other factual statements in my 1963 narrative need retraction on the evidence of British records? Happily, there are but few. My interviewees did me proud. To list those few takes little space:

1. On November 9, 1962, as nobody I saw on either side of the Atlantic remembered six to eight months later, it was not McNamara who phoned Thorneycroft, as had been planned, but rather Thorneycroft who placed the call. He did so because he was due to leave for the airport at noon, sharp, on his way to make a scheduled speech. Since noon was only 7:00 AM in Washington, he feared lest McNamara might be "late" calling him.

Thorneycroft spoke from his office, with his Private Secretary, Arthur Hockaday, in attendance (if not, indeed, on the other phone: Hockaday shortly would send back from the airport a detailed minute of the transatlantic conversation for the private offices at the FO and Admiralty House, Macmillan's temporary workplace). Where did McNamara speak from, somewhat before seven? Very possibly his office, or alternatively his car, if still en route, and in all events alone, no doubt taken slightly by surprise since he'd assumed it was his call to place.

Who phoned whom is but a tiny shade of difference. But it is quite enough to underscore their different memories of the ways they did (or didn't) treat the term "Polaris."

2. Thorneycroft's next trip, which was to Bonn, long scheduled, explains the timing of his first face-to-face discussion with the PM. That did not occur until November 20, 1962, some three days after his return. It also explains the timing of London's communication with its embassy in Washington. While awaiting Thorneycroft, Macmillan and Home sought two things from their Ambassador, the President's friend, David Ormsby Gore. On November 14 they asked whether the PM should phone the President. Gore responded on November 18 with a reasoned "no." Then, as an outgrowth of the PM's meeting of November 20, a cable went to Gore requesting him to seek from JFK the "procedural" assurances which were to guard against premature publicity. Gore responded affirmatively on November 21, with what he thought were those assurances.[4] (They were the ones that Kennedy indeed gave Gore but neglected to mention to anyone else.)

My report of 1963 rolls these requests together, under the first and last of those four dates—November 15 (a day late) and 21—observing of Gore's response, "It took him a week, which is interesting in itself." As the Introduction to this book has noted, in 1963 Gore was my only British reader. In subsequent discussion, those were the words to which he took chief exception. No wonder!

My narrative also expressed uncertainty about the meaning of some time lags after November 9. The British record makes it plain that busy Londoners with preset schedules needed a full ten days before they could get together. But they were at proper pains to cover their flank in the interim.

The November 20 meeting with Macmillan was no casual affair. It included the Foreign Secretary, Home, the Lord Privy Seal, Heath (then housed at the Foreign Office to conduct the EEC negotiations in Brussels), and—sticky or not—Chief of Defence Staff, Admiral, Lord Mountbatten. They canvassed the situation thoroughly, the prospects for Skybolt and the feasible alternatives, Polaris in the lead. The group concluded by agreeing, first, that those procedural assurances should be obtained from Washington, and second, that the Ministry of Defence should prepare a costed program for an alternative system before McNamara's contemplated visit. A "practicable and acceptable alternative should have been worked out in enough detail to enable Her Majesty's Government to propose it for adoption" (and perhaps for simultaneous announcement).[5]

How McNamara would have cheered those words! On paper they do not seem in the least like "immobility." Rather, they seem precisely like what he and his four colleagues at the White House on November 7 had expected of the "clever chaps" in London: They would come up with what they wanted, cost it out, decide upon it, and present it as theirs when McNamara arrived. Of course, nothing like that happened.

Those words were never translated from paper to accomplished fact.

After "prolonged discussion in this department and with others . . . in the Nuclear Deterrent Study Group" (a relatively walled-off body, it appears), Thorneycroft sent Macmillan a minute on December 7, noting that it was "not an agreed paper, but put up mainly on my own responsibility."[6] This sketched an alternative to Skybolt in bare outline: seven British-built Polaris submarines with dual capability as hunter-killers—which, it seems, the Navy wanted anyway, somehow, sometime—carrying eight missiles apiece, not the American 16, the missiles to be purchased from the States but their warheads British. The subs would be constructed in the United Kingdom under stretched-out (cheaper) production schedules. These would see the group complete only in 1974. That would be some eight or nine years after the present airborne force began to lose its credibility as a nuclear deterrent. To fill the gap, perhaps the United States could be brought to rent some two or three American Polaris subs, their missiles equipped with British warheads.

Accompanying this formulation was the very rough comparative-cost estimate which Thorneycroft shared with the PM before McNamara arrived and then with the latter, late in their meeting. It is what left McNamara thinking, as he later told me, that "they hadn't done a thing!"[7]

Immobility is a relative concept. Compared to the charge from the meeting of November 20, this was thin stuff, scarcely suitable for presentation to the Cabinet, or decision, or for formal presentation as the British plan to Washington, let alone the public. From McNamara's standpoint, that thin stuff amounted to nothing. He wanted a firm British position, approved and set to go. But compared to my characterization of Thorneycroft's behavior in the chapter of my 1963 report titled "Thorneycroft Keeps Quiet," this seems "noisy" indeed. Had McNamara brought the word that he could have a straight swap of Polaris for Skybolt, that paper on dual-capability subs and projected rentals should have sufficed to focus both their minds on the next step of a Navy-to-Navy task force, its priorities and subcommittees, and to fence off "rent" as something special. December 11, 1962, could then have been for both of them a reasonably productive day.

Judging from British records, I'd have done better to title that chapter "Thorneycroft Prepares Quietly under Constraints."

McNamara voiced his complaint, "nothing," to so many besides me, in the winter of 1962–63, that it got into the journalistic record and has stood ever since as something for British historians to challenge. Once the files were opened after 1992, they discovered not only the grand Cabinet–committee–level meeting of November 20, but also the less grand, if more effortful work on hunter-killer subs and American rentals.[8] So the Brits were not "immobilized"! Well, literally no. Another plus for them. But from McNamara's standpoint the story remains the same. And so it does from mine, immobility being relative.

Allowing for the marginal involvement of Mountbatten, the British files suggest that Thorneycroft's constraints were as I described them, only more so, while his aims, from time to time in 1962, were much as he and Hockaday told me of them, eight months later.[9] The same can be said for Macmillan, as described to me by Messrs. Bligh and de Zulueta.[10]

II

What I find fascinating in the British files is not the occasional corrected fact—as above—but rather the continued opportunities for enrichment of the basic story. The thrust remains the same: The terms of McNamara's warning of November 7 kept the British from behaving as he wished them to do, and as they would have done had they known Skybolt was definitively gone. Instead they waited, with concern but hope, for him either to back away or to offer them Polaris. But how wonderfully embellished with corroborative detail and ironic twists the narrative becomes when one adds British records to the interviews from which I worked!

The story grows richer in numbers of particulars. Thorneycroft's degree of quietude is one example, but by no means the most interesting. More interesting, at least to me, are those that would especially have struck President Kennedy, enlivening my narrative, hence easing my task of keeping him reading. There are, I think, six of those richest enrichers embedded in British records.

The first enriching item I would mention is buried in the minute Arthur Hockaday sent the FO and the PM's Private Office, reporting Thorneycroft's phone call to McNamara on November 9. According to Hockaday, McNamara specifically mentioned Polaris among the alternatives, were Skybolt to be canceled. Whereupon Thorneycroft was "at pains to stress the need for any agreed alternative, whether Polaris or other, to have the same degree of independence as Skybolt. Mr McNamara took this point." [11] So the latter got a telephonic version in November of the eloquent speech on "independence" Thorneycroft gave face-to-face (and John Rubel wrote down) on December 11.

But if Adam Yarmolinsky, McNamara's then assistant, is to be believed —and why not?—our Secretary of Defense may have taken the point but didn't get it, didn't understand what he was told, until he returned from Paris in mid-December and was briefed by Yarmolinsky on the actual terms of the 1960 Camp David agreement: Skybolt (if developed and produced) would be available to Britain without strings. Having come to office almost two years later, by which time the British bomber force was targeted with SAC, McNamara may have connected that targeting to NATO, assumed an initial assignment, and thought it an original condition—with Polaris assigned to NATO an equivalent. If so, he could not hear what Thorneycroft was telling him.

In Chapter 2 above, my report makes a point of this, with respect to the meeting of December 11 and after. But by then the crisis, and something like its Nassau resolution, were nearly inevitable. Given Hockaday's wordage, the point needs making much earlier in the story, with respect to the calm phone call of November 9. Had McNamara recently or ever read the Camp David language? Almost surely not. Could Thorneycroft have guessed that McNamara hadn't? Again, almost surely not. Thorneycroft himself, no doubt, had the language at his fingertips, and no doubt would have quoted it, over and over, had he conceived the need.

So here's another transatlantic misunderstanding, a probable, not a certain one, but if correctly stated perhaps enough to explain all—and rooted, just as with the rest, in unperceived shades of institutional difference. Thorneycroft had not been at Camp David either. Why do I assume he knew that language? Because, for one thing, it embodied policy, and the PM's at that, squarely in the center of his departmental duties. And for another thing, his Private Office would have had the instinct and the means to call the documents up from ministry files. Whereas in McNamara's case, not only was the policy at issue, but his personal assistant was still improvising a new role—and the documents were nowhere at the Pentagon. Having originated in the White House and remaining there through 1960, they (being the President's) had gone with Eisenhower to retirement at Gettysburg, Pennsylvania.[12]

Yarmolinsky is perhaps to be congratulated for retrieving those files as early as December. Yet had he done so a month sooner, my story's shape might have been altogether changed. So Hockaday's words suggest. Kennedy would have seen that in a flash.

Hockaday's November minute also is the prime source for my second matter of enrichment. He very fully reported McNamara's cover-story, warning now as though decision had not yet been reached: A serious review was underway. There were continuing troubles with the Skybolt missile's guidance system, cost overruns, prospective future outlays of $2.5 billion. For American needs, there was comparative advantage in Minuteman. The issue had just been referred to the Joint Chiefs of Staff for their views. These, when received, would trigger McNamara's own last look, and then final review by the President, with decision some five weeks off—Gore already had reported that it would be taken in four—all subject to more talk about a substitute for Britain, if Skybolt failed to make it through those hurdles.[13]

All this was literally true—except the five-week interval (McNamara mentioned as decision date what he privately had guessed would be the probable leak date). Yet, given what my report shows had happened and would happen in Washington, it was also decidedly misleading. Judged from their files, the British were misled, none more than the Prime Minister.

Hockaday's quotes were so unvarnished and so detailed that they at once became the template for reality most Londoners laid on Washington. Understandably they took the decision as still unmade—or tentative— and those yet-to-do reviews as possible entry points for Skybolt's British friends. On the record, Macmillan saw it so from first to last, until he got to Nassau and read Kennedy's TV remarks on Skybolt. Even Gore in Washington scarcely saw it differently, and embassy reportage kept lending credence to British visions of those reviews.

Thorneycroft, who had actually heard spoken the words Hockaday reported, judged personally, from then on, as he told me the next summer, that Skybolt was a goner.[14] But he could scarcely rise in meetings and call McNamara a liar, his reviews but false fronts for decisions already taken. Possibly they weren't.

McNamara had been too clever for his own good, and too detailed about procedure. As Chapter 2 shows, he wanted Thorneycroft and the PM to grasp that the decision was really made, but in such terms as to keep that disguised for two weeks from his own Chiefs of Staff. His words, as rendered by Gore and then Hockaday, disguised it also, for a longer time, from Admiralty House, the British Services, Defence officialdom, and the FO!

My third matter of enrichment stems from British embassy reportage in November and December 1962. Mostly it was very good indeed. The Defence and Air Force attachés, and the special Skybolt office (created to monitor development) did yeoman work in keeping their parts of London informed. Long before November 8, the MOD had ample reason to be worried about Skybolt's future. That everyone appropriate was worried, the files leave in no doubt. This specifically included Thorneycroft, whose subtle, cautionary message to McNamara on November 5 led directly to the latter's meeting with the President on November 7 and with the British Ambassador the next day. Gore's report of McNamara's warning was exemplary, though naturally interpreted by light of Hockaday's minute on the succeeding conversation with Thorneycroft.

From then on, Gore answered every inquiry with promptness, while his military aides reported every scrap of gossip they could get out of the Pentagon. In two respects, both curious, they seen to have contributed to London's misreading of Washington's likely intent. Gore himself is responsible for the one, his military aides, uncorrected by him, for the other.

The first of these is found in Gore's cable of November 18, 1962, regarding the question of a phone call from the PM to the President. Elaborating on his reasons for "no further approach at this time," Gore wrote "I have no doubt that the President and McNamara have been fully aware of the political importance to us of Skybolt. Indeed it could hardly be otherwise after what had been said to them directly by successive Ministers of Defence and the Prime Minister." [15] Gore returned to this theme as late as December 8, writing the Foreign Secretary, who passed it to the PM, "the President himself . . . is a highly developed political animal and is acutely aware of the political implications." [16] In fact, that acute awareness was still to come, ten days later, on JFK's plane ride to Nassau with Gore. But Home had been convinced of American awareness long since, and would remain so until December 11.

As early as November 8, seeking help to press the case for Skybolt before they even got word of the McNamara warning—which shows how little they needed that—Thorneycroft had written Home in the same vein, recalling that when in the States in September, "I told Mr. McNamara it would be a catastrophe for us if Skybolt programs were scrapped. The implications go wider than defence. Cancellation would have a profoundly disturbing effect upon the attitude to America on the Conservative Back Bench." [17]

So, emulating Americans at the White House and Defense, these Londoners supposed that their allies across the water heard what they were saying in the same terms they were saying it, and never sought the feedback that might have shown them wrong. Instead, they kept on saying it, while telling one another, as a form of reassurance, how elegantly they had done so.

As a second problem with its reports, the British embassy for some reason failed to pick up lack of unanimity in the American Joint Chiefs of Staff. From late November, British military aides reported gleefully and often that the Chiefs were against Skybolt cancellation, but neglected to say—because presumably they did not know—that General Taylor, Chairman of the Chiefs, supported it. Disinformation by the U.S. Air Force may have been the cause.

Regardless of the cause, as late as December 12, 1962, this made it possible for the Prime Minister to write his Private Secretary, de Zulueta, from whom he was briefly separated, "I am still rather in favor of sending . . . [the Americans] . . . a technical report by our advisers [on Skybolt feasibility]. This document if it were published or leaked, would be a very hard blow to the Administration. The American Chiefs of Staff would demand continuation of Skybolt. . . . I therefore think this is a weapon which we ought not to neglect. . . . we must have copies available when we go to the Bahamas." [18] In the event they didn't, no such report having been written, and once he got there Macmillan promptly gave up Skybolt. But that he could have contemplated such a tactic less than a week before is testimony not alone to his continued preference for the status quo, but also to that gap in embassy reporting.

The fourth matter of enrichment I find striking leaps from the files of the Secretary of State for Air. He was then, as I somehow failed to remind President Kennedy, that formidable Scot and war hero Hugh Fraser, leader of the "Suez Group," for long a very visible back-bencher on the Tory right, a chief potential instigator of the catastrophe against which Thorneycroft warned, quite capable of going over the latter's head to the Prime Minister. Fraser was a devotee of every Air Force cause, passionately pro-Skybolt, deeply suspicious of such scientists as Solly Zuckerman.

Here was a nominally subordinate minister, not in the Cabinet, with plenty of time on his hands and great aptitude for writing cautionary memos to the Secretary of State for Defence—which he did on average perhaps once a week, often enough copying them to Admiralty House, Macmillan's temporary quarters.

Every one of the constraints internal to Thorneycroft's Ministry of Defence, as cataloged in Chapter 2, is heightened by and takes on added color from the personalization of the RAF in Fraser. President Kennedy might well have supplied the name for himself, and intuited much of its burdensome meaning, to his own wry amusement at Thorneycroft's plight. But I regret not having inserted the name, and I regret still more that I could not have used Fraser's files for illustrative quotes. There are many.

For instance, on October 16, 1962, commenting on warnings from the attachés in Washington, Fraser wrote Thorneycroft, "Our deterrent depends entirely on Skybolt . . . on this there can be absolutely no question. . . . no alternative at this stage." (He also complained about the alleged wickedness of Solly Zuckerman in Washington.)[19]

On November 11, two days after McNamara's warning, Fraser wrote Thorneycroft that until it was demonstrated by the Americans themselves that the British couldn't talk them out of canceling Skybolt, "we should take great care that the method and timing of [British] examination of alternatives do not prejudice our chances" to do so.[20] This is something Thorneycroft plainly took to heart. Fraser also thought Sir Robert Scott, the Permanent Secretary, should call off a scheduled MOD-wide meeting of officials where discussion of alternatives would be appropriate. Apparently that was done. The Nuclear Deterrent Study Group which Thorneycroft consulted was, by far, a more restricted venue.

On November 14, Fraser sent word to Thorneycroft reminding him that he had promised to get Home to seek Gore's views on when the PM should step in. The Air attaché was now reporting that JCS examination "is due to be completed November 16." Over the weekend it seemed possible that McNamara would be advising Kennedy: "There therefore may be need to ask the Prime Minister to intervene earlier than we supposed." Thorneycroft, briefly back from visitations, may then have been the spur for Home's telegram of the same date to Gore. In all events, Fraser added his view "that both the Foreign Secretary and the Prime Minister should be aware . . . there is no means of providing a credible, independent British deterrent between 1965–66 and 1969–70 from within our own resources, if Skybolt is denied to us."[21] He then sent copies to Admiralty House, to the FO, and to the Minister of Aviation, Julian Amery, Macmillan's son-in-law, a deeply interested spectator. The message to Gore was duly dispatched—as perhaps it would have been anyway.

On November 29, Fraser again wrote Thorneycroft, this time to cite an embassy dispatch: "I am personally much encouraged by the fact that the JCS have unanimously reported in favor of Skybolt. . . . This is a card I believe we should play to the limit." [22] The advice rolled off Thorneycroft's back, but perhaps not the Prime Minister's.

Some days before December 11, at about the time Thorneycroft prepared his minute for Macmillan on what he proposed to say to McNamara, he heard further from his Secretary for Air. In an undated paper Fraser wrote that upon meeting the American, Thorneycroft would find it "vital to display no sign of weakness and decline to consider alternatives to Skybolt until every possible pressure had been brought to bear"—including pressure by Prime Minister on President. Fraser noted further, "I am sending a copy of this minute to the PM." [23]

And some days after December 11, Fraser wrote again, ostensibly to critique McNamara's aide-mémoire. The Air Minister dismissed technical difficulties with Skybolt as "typical of teething troubles," and, in an appendix, dismissed Hound Dog as unsuitable. But the heart of Fraser's criticism lay elsewhere. "In the eyes of the world," he asked rhetorically, are "hired" submarines until the 1970s an adequate substitute for a flexible bomber force? Two subs permanently on station, meaning three in rotation: "laughable," he wrote, "in the eyes of the world." [24]

By the time this came to Thorneycroft he had already been warned by McNamara, at a quiet tête-à-tête in Paris, that renting subs from the Americans would be extremely difficult. At the heart of the difficulty lay Admiral Hyman Rickover, father, boss, and guardian of the nuclear submarine program for the U.S. Navy. As Gore wrote at about the same time, the Admiral "has almost as violent an antipathy for the British Navy as for his own." [25] But that was the least of it. Rickover was determined to keep foreigners of every sort away from the secrets of quiet propulsion in American Polaris subs. This is why Robert Bowie's projected mixed-manned MLF, originally conceived as comprising just such submarines, had suddenly been reconceived in the United States as surface freighters steaming to and fro: Rickover had set his face against the other. McNamara did not care to go into that detail, but he and others did convince the British that at Nassau they would be well advised to drop the rental part of their alternative. So they did. Fraser's threatened laughter (in the House of Commons?) may have contributed. Better a gap than that.

How such quotations vivify the ministerial constraints upon the British Defence Secretary! When one adds the constraints from above him, from the Treasury as usual and, more important, from the PM, preferring, as Macmillan did, the status quo (which had his name on it), Thorneycroft's words to me the following July take on immediacy and poignancy. The sharpest of those are quoted in my Memorandum of Conversation dated

July 30, 1963: "I knew Bob was going to scrap this thing . . . But I could not step out until the Americans had made a move. I could not express to my own people or in public a preference for Polaris until I was sure I could get it. . . . I couldn't appear to be in the position of backing away from Skybolt myself as a voluntary act in the eyes of my own people, nor did I want to start a negotiation on my knees. So I had to wait for McNamara to make the move."

My fifth item of enrichment emerges from the British minutes of the Nassau Conference and related papers, as compared with American counterparts. I wrote my 1963 report from the latter (which are generally more colorful, reflecting national characteristics, perhaps, but also authorship by McGeorge Bundy, no mean stylist). Style aside, when one sees both it becomes clear that for most, perhaps all British participants, Nassau seemed a harder, chancier, and more drawn-out encounter than it did for the best informed Americans, those closest to the President. The latter group believed—and as I read their record I agree—that Kennedy knew he would have to concede Polaris to Macmillan on the latter's then terms, either when they took their walk on the evening of December 18, or at the latest when the PM finished his extraordinary presentation the next morning: "We will go on and make [the Polaris system ourselves] and be free. . . . better than putting a British sailor aboard ship to have tea with the Portuguese."

Thereafter, Bundy among others was persuaded, as I recall he told me, that the President saw no other option.[26] He would delay a bit and let his people see what they could do by way of argument and a restrictive draft communiqué—shades of Rusk with his people, and McNamara with Rusk's on December 11—but if Macmillan held firm, Kennedy would give him what he felt he had to have: Polaris assigned to NATO with a worldwide escape clause.

Reading the British minutes and memoranda leaves a rather different impression, namely that after his exertions on December 19, Macmillan was discouraged by that U.S. draft communiqué, which seemed to deny him an escape clause of the very sort he needed. If the PM had some presidential hint to make him feel better, he didn't show it. To the rump Cabinet in London he cabled the next morning, "I am afraid things are not at present going very well. . . . So far the Americans have felt unwilling to offer us [Polaris] on terms that are acceptable. . . . We are going to try again tomorrow . . . but I do not know how far we will be successful.[27]

Macmillan enclosed a British draft communiqué in case the Americans wouldn't yield: ". . . The PM recognizes with regret that the US decision inevitably marked the end of a period of close Anglo-American cooperation in which he himself has always believed. . . . The UK should now make a determined effort to build not only their own submarines and warheads but their own missiles, so that the independent British power which has always been used in the spirit of the alliance should not disappear." Painful for Kennedy, a pleasure to de Gaulle, a rallying cry for Tories: that draft, seemingly, has Thorneycroft's fingerprints on it as well as Macmillan's.

Indeed, as Chapter 2 shows, the Defence Minister was all for flying out of there without more ado, leaving that communiqué behind. Late on the 19th, even as he was still being "sat on" by Gore and Duncan Sandys, Thorneycroft wrote the PM that

> having studied the American draft communiqué and annexes, . . .
>
> 4. Given that these documents reflect the real attitude of the [American] Administration, I am strongly against any attempt to find a formula which glosses over the very deep and wide chasm between us. Even if such . . . could be found, it would lead to public disagreements on the interpretation.
> 5. Public reactions in Britain are easy to forecast. We shall be accused of spending vast sums of the taxpayers' money to create a force not under our control in order to subscribe it to NATO. . . .[28]

On December 21, when the two sides met again for formal talks on Skybolt and alternatives, Macmillan made another speech, incorporating precisely those themes. Shortly after, the Americans conceded. Sat on or not, his Defence Minister had served him somewhat as Thorneycroft himself had sometimes been served by Fraser.

My sixth and last enrichment found in the British files comes not from any single set of documents, but rather from many, scattered through the whole, which show how differently the British and most Americans perceived what they and we were arguing about.

For one thing, to most members of the Kennedy administration, Skybolt and Polaris were quite different matters, the latter a great departure. To the British they were equally familiar and as linked as salt and pepper, although to be used sequentially, not both at the same time. As early as 1960, at and after Camp David, once the British had opted for Skybolt (cheaper and more wanted by the Air Force than Polaris by the Navy), Harold Watkinson, Thorneycroft's predecessor, had tried hard for a further American commitment of Polaris as the follow-on weapon for the 1970s. He failed to get it promised without NATO strings, in the form of a multinational precursor of the MLF about which the Americans were talking even then, in Eisenhower's time. But ever since, at MOD, the Royal Navy, even

Admiralty House, even the RAF, it seems to have been taken for granted that if they were to retain their deterrent after Skybolt ceased deterring, circa 1969, they would have to succeed, somehow, where Watkinson had failed.

For another thing, by early 1962 the British saw their deterrent not as an independent constraint on Moscow, but rather as a means to persuade Washington that London made an "independent [sometimes phrased "significant"] . . . contribution to the strategic nuclear deterrent of the West." So, at least, the Treasury was told, to head off raids on V-bombers in compensation for the prospective costs of Skybolt acquisition.[29] From that persuasion flowed British membership in the "Nuclear Club"—as McGeorge Bundy once remarked to me, "the most expensive status symbol since colonies"—and chances for Macmillan credibly to press, on Washington and Moscow both, his deep concern with disarmament.

And for a final thing, the British files elaborate somewhat the difference Rubel's notes so well captured between McNamara and Thorneycroft on December 11. It is the difference between nuclear missiles as weapons for war and as symbols for discourse in politics. Throughout the upper reaches of the British government, everyone apparently conceived them in the latter sense. Macmillan set the tone and took the lead in this. By comparison in Washington, from McNamara down, most members of the Pentagon, and not a few at State, some even in the White House—not to mention Congress—thought of nuclears as possibly useful in actual wars, with conventional forces as more flexible, safer substitutes.

In April 1962, six months before the Cuban missile crisis, Macmillan met with McNamara for what turned out to be an extraordinary dialogue of the deaf, although Berlin was the ostensible subject. It would have taken Bundy to do justice to their interchange, but even in the bland, spare language of the British minute, the differences between them on both sorts of forces stand out sharply.

For the PM, veteran of two World Wars, now serving as chief minister of a small, vulnerable island, any war engulfing Europe, conventional or nuclear, was the ultimate failure of policy, the end of politics. With the approach of "mutual assured destruction," nuclear war could no longer be an option for sane people, while conventional war in Europe was equally unsuitable, at least for Europeans. Reducing armaments gave sanity more chance. Once Berlin was settled, should that not be tried?

Whereas for McNamara, dutiful and rational to a fault—a World War II Air Force statistical controller, subsequently president of the Ford Motor Company—warfare was his present business, with conventional options much preferred and disarmament distrusted, lest its advocacy send enemies wrong signals, at least until conventional rearmament had been completed.[30]

By December 1962, three months after the Cuban crisis—if not, indeed, before—President Kennedy was privately more Macmillanite than McNamarian. The evidence of White House tapes made during the crisis seems overwhelming on that score.[31] This was part of the bond between those two chiefs of government, JFK and the PM, part of the way they viewed the human condition, wryly, with an underlay of tragedy, part of the reason that the former treated the latter's pleas with more consideration than Macmillan himself may have expected.

Had I been allowed in London, as I was in Washington, to read everybody's files before I interviewed them, I now know that I would have kept my story much the same, a marvelous piece of mirror-imaging on each side of the water, simultaneously. But fleshing out the detail on the British side would have made the story both more complicated and more interesting. This, however, does not change my comparative evaluation: In terms of getting something close to what he wanted on his government's behalf, Macmillan did better than Kennedy. He did so partly because his was the reactive role, not the initiatory one. Partly the PM did so because, relatively speaking, his government worked better.

Placing that judgment in context calls for a turn to comparative institutions. Chapter 4 reprints a paper, subsequently published on both sides of the Atlantic, I initially drafted in 1964, the summer after my Skybolt study, to characterize and compare our "Presidential" system with their "Cabinet" government (not wholly to the latter's advantage it turned out). The comparison is contemporary, roughly, with the happenings recounted in Chapters 2 and 3. Alas, institutions don't stand still, emphatically not these, so lest the reader take the early 1960s to embody the late 1990s, I have added Chapter 5, contrasting "then" with "now."

4

White House and Whitehall (1964)

[This chapter reprints a paper with the same title, initially drafted in 1964 and redrafted in 1965 for presentation to the Annual Meeting of the American Political Science Association. It was subsequently published, with minor deletions, in *The Public Interest* (Winter 1966) and republished, with deletions restored, in Anthony King, ed., *The British Prime Minister* (London: Macmillan, 1969).]

"Cabinet Government," so-called, as practiced currently in the United Kingdom, differs in innumerable ways, some obvious, some subtle, from "Presidential Government" in the United States. To ask what one can learn about our own machine by viewing theirs—which is the question posed for me—may seem farfetched, considering those differences. But actually the question is a good one. For the differences are matters of degree and not of kind.

Despite surface appearances these two machines, the British and American, are not now at opposite poles. Rather they are somewhat differently located near the center of a spectrum stretching between ideal types, from collective leadership to one-man rule. Accordingly, a look down Whitehall's corridors of power should suggest a lot of things worth noticing in Washington. At any rate, that is the premise of this paper.

For a President-watcher, who tries to understand the inner politics of our machine and its effects on policy by climbing inside now and then and learning on the job, it is no easy matter to attempt comparison with the internal life of Whitehall. How is one to get a comparable look? Those who govern Britain mostly keep their secrets to themselves. They rarely have incentive to do otherwise, which is among the differences between us. Least of all are they inclined to satisfy curiosities of *academics*, especially not English academics. But even we colonials, persistent though we are and mattering as little as we do, find ourselves all too frequently treated like Englishmen and kept at bay by those three magic words, "Official Secrets Act." Why not? Nothing in the British Constitution says that anyone outside of Whitehall needs an inside view. Quite the reverse. If academics knew, then journalists might learn, and even the back-benchers might find out. God forbid! That could destroy the Constitution. Governing is *meant* to be a mystery.

And so it is, not only in the spoken words of those who do it but also, with rare exceptions, in the written words of journalists and scholars. Only in the memoirs of participants does one get glimpses now and then of operational reality. And even the most "indiscreet" of recent memoirs veil the essence of the modern system: the relations between ministers and civil servants in the making of a government decision.[1] Former civil servants have at least as great a stake as former ministers in shielding those relationships: the stake of loyalty to their own professional successors in the governing of Britain. What could matter more than that?

For four years I have made a hobby of attempting to poke holes in their defenses, and to take a closer look than either interviews or books afford. Partly this has been a "busman's holiday": having roamed one set of corridors I find it irresistible to look around another set. Partly, though, I have been tempted by the thought that comparison of likenesses and differences would add a new dimension to President-watching.

To test that proposition I have taken every look at Whitehall I could manage by a whole variety of means. Happily for me, White House assignments have contributed to this endeavor. In 1961 when I enjoyed the hospitality of Nuffield College and began my inquiries in Whitehall, the vague status of sometime-Kennedy-consultant opened many doors. It helps to be an object of curiosity. It also helps to have been an official, even in another government: one then "talks shop." In 1963 President Kennedy asked me for a confidential report on the evolution of the Skybolt crisis in both governments. Prime Minister Macmillan co-operated. I learned a lot. In 1964 President Johnson asked me to help facilitate communications between governments in preparation for his first meeting with Harold Wilson as Prime Minister. Wilson then had just come into office. Whitehall was in transition. Again, I learned a lot. Each time I go to London now I learn a little more.

If this strikes you as a hard way, or an odd way, to do "research," I should simply say that I have found no better way to study bureaucratic politics. While the specifics of official business remain classified, perceptions of behavior in the doing of the business become grist for our academic mill. I shall draw on such perceptions in this paper. You will understand, of course, that I am still a novice Whitehallologist. It would take ten years of such "research" before I came to trust my own perceptions. This, perforce, is but an interim report on insufficient evidence from an unfinished study.

What I shall do here is to raise two simple points of difference between their machine and ours, with an eye to implications for the study of *our* system:

First, we have counterparts for their top civil servants—but not in our own civil service.

Second, we have counterparts for their Cabinet ministers—but not exclusively or even mainly in our Cabinet.

If I state these two correctly, and I think I do, it follows that in our conventional comparisons we students all too often have been victims of semantics. Accordingly, in our proposals for reform-by-analogy (a favorite sport of the American Political Science Association since its founding) we all too often have confused function with form. I find no functions in the British system for which ours lacks at least nascent counterparts. But it is rare when institutions with the same names in both systems do the same work for precisely the same purpose. We make ourselves much trouble, analytically, by letting nomenclature dictate our analogies. I hope this paper offers something of an antidote.

For the most important things that I bring back from my excursioning in Whitehall are a question and a caution. The question: what is our functional equivalent? The caution: never base analysis on nomenclature. With these I make my case for a comparative approach to American studies. These seem to be embarrassingly obvious. But that is not the way it works in practice. By way of illustration let me take in turn those "simple" points of difference between Whitehall and Washington.

I

"Why are your officials so passionate?" I once was asked in England by a bright young Treasury official just back from Washington. I inquired with whom he had been working there; his answer "Your chaps at the Budget Bureau."

To an American those "chaps" appear to be among the most dispassionate of Washingtonians. Indeed, the Budget staff traditionally prides itself on being cool, collected, and above the struggle, distant from emotions churning in the breasts of importunate agency officials. Yet to my English friend, "They took themselves so seriously . . . seemed to be crusaders for the policy positions they thought made sense . . . seemed to feel that it was up to them to save the day . . ." If this is how the Budget Bureau struck him, imagine how he would have felt about some circles in our Air Force, or the European Bureau of the State Department, or the Office of Economic Opportunity, or the Forest Service, for that matter, or the Bureau of Reclamation, or the National Institutes of Health!

His question is worth pondering, though that is not my purpose here.[2] What I should rather do is to pursue two further questions which his inquiry suggests. First, out of what frame of reference was he asking? And second, is it sensible of him (and most of us) to talk of our own budgeteers as though they were his counterparts? I ask because I think that we are very far from candid with ourselves about the way we get *his* work done in *our* system.

This young man was a Principal-with-prospects at the Treasury. By definition, then, he was a man of the administrative class, elite corps of the British civil service. More importantly, he was also apprentice-member of the favored few, elite-of-the-elite, who climb the ladder *in* the Treasury. With skill and luck and approbation from his seniors he might someday rise to be a mandarin. And meanwhile he would probably serve soon as personal assistant to a Cabinet minister. In short, he had the frame of reference which befits a man whose career ladder rises up the central pillar of the whole Whitehall machine toward the heights where dwell the seniors of all seniors, molders of ministers, heads of the civil service, knights in office, lords thereafter: Permanent Secretaries of the Cabinet and Treasury.

English civil servants of this sort, together with their Foreign Office counterparts, comprise the inner corps of "officials," civilian careerists, whose senior members govern the United Kingdom in collaboration with their ministerial superiors the front-bench politicians, leaders of the parliamentary party which commands a House majority for the time being. Theirs is an intimate collaboration grounded in the interests and traditions of both sides. Indeed it binds them into a Society for Mutual Benefit: what they succeed in sharing with each other they need share with almost no one else, and governing in England is a virtual duopoly.

This is the product of a tacit treaty, an implicit bargain, expressed in self-restraints which are observed on either side. The senior civil servants neither stall nor buck decisions of the government once taken in due form by their political masters. "Due form" means consultation, among other things, but having been consulted these officials act without public complaint or private evasion, even though they may have fought what they are doing up to the last moment of decision. They also try to assure comparable discipline in lower official ranks, and to squeeze out the juniors who do not take kindly to it. The senior politicians, for their part—with rare and transient exceptions—return the favor in full measure.

The politicians rarely meddle with official recruitment or promotion; by and large, officialdom administers itself. They preserve the anonymity of civil servants both in Parliament and in the press. Officials never testify on anything except "accounts," and nobody reveals their roles in shaping public policy. Ministers take kudos for themselves, likewise the heat. They also take upon themselves protection for the status of officialdom in the society: honours fall like gentle rain at stated intervals. They even let careerists run their private offices, and treat their personal assistants of the moment (detailed from civil service ranks) as confidentially as our department heads treat trusted aides imported from outside. More importantly, the politicians *lean* on their officials. They *expect* to be advised. Most importantly, they very often do what they are told, and follow the advice that they receive.

This is an advantageous bargain for both sides. It relieves the politicians of a difficult and chancy search for "loyal" advisers and administrators. These are there, in place, ready to hand. And it relieves officials of concern for their security in terms both of profession and of person. No wonder our careerists appear "passionate" to one of theirs; they have nothing at stake in Britain except policy!

So a Treasury-type has everything to gain by a dispassionate stance, and nothing to lose except arguments. Since he is an elitist, ranking intellectually and morally with the best in Britain, this is no trifling loss. If parliamentary parties were less disciplined than they now are, or if he had back-benchers who identified with him, he could afford to carry arguments outside official channels, as his predecessors sometimes did a century ago, and *military* officers still do, on occasion.[3] But party discipline calls forth its counterpart in his own ranks. And party politicians on back-benches have no natural affinities for *civil* servants—quite the contrary. He really has no recourse but to lose his arguments with grace and wait in patience for another day, another set of ministers. After all, he stays, they go. And while he stays he shares the fascinating game of power, stretching his own mind and talents in the service of a reasonably grateful country.

The Treasury-type is a disciplined man, but a man fulfilled, not frustrated. His discipline is what he pays for power. Not every temperament can take it; if he rises in the Treasury he probably can. Others are weeded out. But there is more to this than a cold compromise for power's sake. Those who rise and find fulfillment in their work do so in part because they are deliberately exposed at mid-career to the constraints, the miseries, the hazards which afflict the human beings who wield power on the political side. They know the lot of ministers from observation at first hand. Exposure makes for empathy and for perspective. It also makes for comfort with the civil servant's lot. Whitehall's elitists gain all three while relatively young. It leaves them a bit weary with the weight of human folly, but it rids them of self-righteousness, the bane of *our* careerists—which is, of course, endemic among budgeteers.

A Treasury-type gains this exposure through that interesting device, the tour of duty in a minister's private office as his personal assistant ("dogsbody" is their term for it). The Private Secretary, so called, now serves his master-of-the-moment as a confidential aide, minding his business, doing his chores, sharing his woes, offering a crying towel, bracing him for bad days in the House, briefing him for bad days in the office. Etcetera. Remarkably, by our standards, the civil service has preempted such assignments for its own. (Do not confuse these with mere *Parliamentary* Private Secretaries.) Still more remarkably, the politicians feel themselves well served and rarely dream of looking elsewhere for the service. I know an instance where a minister confided in his Private Secretary a secret he told no one else save the Prime Minister, not even his Permanent Secretary, the career head-of-department, "lest it embarrass him to know." The Permanent Secretary was the Private Secretary's boss in career terms. Yet the secret was kept as a matter of course. This, I am assured, is not untypical: "ministerial secrets" are all in the day's work for dogsbodies.

Accordingly, the one-time Private Secretary who has risen in due course to be a Permanent Secretary of a department knows far more of what it feels like to perform as politician than his opposite number, the department's minister, can ever hope to fathom in reverse. A William Armstrong, for example, now joint head of the Treasury, whose opposite number is the Chancellor of the Exchequer, spent years as private secretary to a previous Chancellor who was among the ablest men in Cabinets of his time. Consider the ramifications of that![4] And draw the contrast with our own careerists!

Our budgeteers imagine that they are the nearest thing to Treasury civil servants. For this no one can blame them. Much of our literature suggests that if they are not quite the same as yet, a little gimmickry could make them so. Many of our colleagues in this Association have bemused themselves for years with plans to borrow nomenclature and procedures from the British side, on the unstated premise that function follows form. But it does not.

Functionally, our counterparts for British Treasury-types are *non-*careerists holding jobs infused with presidential interest or concern—"in-and-outers" from the law firms, banking, business, academia, foundations, or occasionally journalism, or the entourages of successful Governors and Senators—along with up-and-outers (sometimes up-and-downers) who relinquish, or at least risk, civil service status in the process. Here is the elite-of-the-elite, the upper-crust of *our* "administrative class." These are the men who serve alongside our equivalents for ministers and share in governing. One finds them in the White House and in the *appointive* jobs across the street at the Executive Office Building. One finds them also on the seventh floor of State, and on the third and fourth floors of the Pentagon: these places among others. If they have not arrived as yet, they probably are trying to get in (or up). If they have gone already, they are likely to be back.

Let me take some names at random to suggest the types. First, the prototype of all: Averell Harriman. Second, a handful of the currently employed: David Bell, both Bundys (by their different routes), Wilbur Cohen, Harry McPherson, Paul Nitze. Third, a few fresh "outers" almost certain to be back, somehow, sometime: Kermit Gordon, Theodore Sorensen, Lee White. Fourth, a long-time "outer" who is never back but always in: Clark Clifford. Three of these men got their start as government careerists, two as academics, one in banking, two in law, and two on Capitol Hill. The numbers are but accidents of random choice; the spread is meaningful.

The jobs done by such men as these have no precise equivalents in England; our machinery is too different. For example, McGeorge Bundy as the President's Assistant for National Security Affairs is something more than Principal Private Secretary to the Prime Minister (reserved for rising Treasury-types), a dogsbody-writ-large, and something different from the Secretary of the Cabinet (top of the tree for them), a post "tradition" turns into an almost constitutional position, certainly what we call an "institutional" one. Yet the men in those positions see a Bundy as their sort of public servant. They are higher on the ladder than my young friend with the question; they do not take budgeteers to be their counterparts: they know a Senior Civil Servant when they see one.

A Bundy *is* one in their eyes—and they are right. For so he is in American practice. I mention Bundy whom they actually know. But if they knew a Sorensen, a Moyers, or the like, I have no doubt that they would see them much the same.

Every detail of our practice is un-English, yet the general outline fits. One of our men appears on television; another testifies against a bill; a third and fourth engage in semi-public argument; a fifth man feeds a press campaign to change the President's mind; a sixth disputes a Cabinet member's views in open meeting; a seventh overturns an interagency agreement. So it goes, to the perpetual surprise (and sometimes envy?) of the disciplined duopolists in Britain. Yet by *our* lights, according to *our* standards, under *our* conditions, such activities may be as "disciplined" as theirs, and as responsive to political leadership. The ablest of our in-and-outers frequently display equivalent restraint and equal comprehension in the face of the dilemmas which confront our Presidential counterparts for Cabinet politicians.

The elite of our officialdom is not careerist in the British sense (although, of course, our in-and-outers have careers); why should it be? Neither is the President with his department heads. They too are in-and-outers. We forget that the duopoly which governs Britain is composed of *two* career systems, official and political. Most ministers who will take office through the next decade are on the scene and well identified in Westminster. The Permanent Secretaries who will serve with them are on the Whitehall ladders now; a mere outsider can spot some of them. Contrast our situation—even the directorships of old-line bureaus remain problematical. Who is to succeed J. Edgar Hoover?

We have only two sets of true careerists in our system. One consists of Senators and Congressmen in relatively safe seats, waiting their turn for chairmanships. The other consists of military officers and civil employees who are essentially technicians manning every sort of specialty (including "management") in the Executive establishment. Between these two we leave a lot of room for in-and-outers. We are fortunate to do so. Nothing else could serve as well to keep the two apart. And *their* duopoly would be productive not of governance but of its feudal substitute, piecemeal administration. We can only hope to govern in our system by and through the Presidency. In-and-outers are a saving grace for Presidents.

II

Since 1959, English commentators frequently have wondered to each other if their government was being "presidentialised." In part this stemmed from electoral considerations following the "personality contest" between Harold Macmillan and Hugh Gaitskell at that year's general election. In part it stemmed from operational considerations in the wake of Macmillan's active Premiership—reinforced this past year by the sight of still another activist in office, Harold Wilson.

Despite their differences of style, personality, and party, both Macmillan and Wilson patently conceived the Cabinet Room in Downing Street to be the PM's office, not a mere board room. Both evidently acted on the premise that the PM's personal judgment ought, if possible, to rule the day. Both reached out for the power of personal decision on the issues of the day. Macmillan did so through off-stage maneuver, while avowing his fidelity to Cabinet consensus as befits a man beset by the conventions of committee government. With perhaps a bit more candor, Wilson does the same. But what alerts the commentators is that both have done it. Hence discussion about trends toward presidential government.

Yet between these two Prime Ministers there was another for a year, Sir Alec Douglas-Home. And by no stretch of the imagination could his conduct of the office have been characterized as presidential. On the contrary, by all accounts he was a classic "chairman of the board," who resolutely pushed impending issues *out* of Number 10, for initiative elsewhere by others. He managed, it is said, to get a lot of gardening done while he resided there. I once asked a close observer what became of the initiatives, the steering, the maneuvering, which Home refused to take upon himself. He replied:

> When ministers discovered that he really wouldn't do it, they began to huddle with each other, little groups of major figures. You would get from them enough agreement or accommodation to produce the main lines of a government position, something they could try to steer through Cabinet. Or if you didn't get it, there was nothing to be done. That's how it began to work, outside of Number 10, around it.

That is how it would be working now, had there been a slight shift in the popular vote of 1964.

The British system, then, has *not* been presidentialized, or not at least in operational terms. For as we learned with Eisenhower, the initiatives a President must take to form "the main lines of a government position" cannot be kept outside the White House precincts. Toss them out and either they bounce back or they do not get taken. A president may delegate to White House aides ("ok, S.A."), or to a Foster Dulles, but only as he demonstrates consistently, day-in-and-out, that they command his ear and hold his confidence. Let him take to his bed behind an oxygen tent and they can only go through motions. Eisenhower's White House was a far cry from

10 Downing Street in the regime of Douglas-Home. That remains the distance Britain's system has to travel toward a presidential status for Prime Ministers.

But even though the system did not make an activist of Douglas-Home, his predecessor and successor obviously relished the part. The system may not have required it but they pursued it, and the system bore the weight of their activity. In externals Number 10 looks no more like the White House under Wilson than it did a year ago. But in essence Wilson comes as close to being "President" as the conventions of his system allow. He evidently knows it and likes it. So, I take it, did Macmillan.

How close can such men come? How nearly can they assert "Presidential" leadership inside a Cabinet system? Without endeavoring to answer in the abstract, let me record some impressions of concrete performances.

First, consider Britain's bid for Common Market membership four years ago, which presaged an enormous (if abortive) shift in public policy, to say nothing of Tory Party policy. By all accounts this "turn to Europe" was Macmillan's own. The timing and the impetus were his, and I am told that his intention was to go whole-hog, both economically and politically. As such this was among the great strategic choices in the peacetime politics of Britain. But it never was a Government Decision. For those, by British definition, come in Cabinet. Macmillan never put the issue there in terms like these. Instead he tried to sneak past opposition there—and on back-benches and in constituencies—by disguising his strategic choice as a commercial deal. The Cabinet dealt with issues of negotiation, *en principe* and later in detail, for making Britain part of Europe's economic union without giving up its Commonwealth connections (or farm subsidies). One minister explained to me:

> Timing is everything. First we have to get into the Common Market as a matter of business, good for our economy. Then we can begin to look at the political side. . . . Appetites grow with eating. We couldn't hold the Cabinet, much less our back-benchers, if we put this forward now in broader terms. . . .

Accordingly, the move toward Europe had to be played out in its ostensible terms, as a detailed negotiation of commercial character. This took two years, and while the tactic served its purpose within Tory ranks these were the years when France escaped from the Algerian war. By the time negotiations neared their end, Charles de Gaulle was riding high at home. Macmillan tiptoed past his own internal obstacles, but took so long about it that his path was blocked by an external one, the veto of de Gaulle.

Second, take the Nassau Pact of 1962, which calmed the Skybolt crisis between Washington and London even as it gave de Gaulle excuses for that veto. Macmillan was his own negotiator at the Nassau Conference. He decided on the spot to drop his claim for Skybolt missiles and to press the substitution of Polaris weaponry. He wrung what seemed to him an advantageous compromise along those lines from President Kennedy. Then and only then did he "submit" its terms to the full Cabinet for decision (by return cable), noting the concurrence of three potent ministers who had accompanied him: the Foreign, Commonwealth, and Defence Secretaries. With the President waiting, the Cabinet "decided" (unenthusiastically by all accounts) to bless this virtual *fait accompli*. What else was there to do? The answer, nothing—and no doubt Macmillan knew it.

Third, consider how the present Labour government reversed its pre-election stand on Nassau's terms. Within six weeks of taking office Wilson and his colleagues became champions of the Polaris program they had scorned in Opposition. Their back-benchers wheeled around behind them almost to a man. It is no secret that the PM was the source of this reversal, also its tactician. So far as I can find, it was his own choice, his initiative, his management, from first to last. He got it done in quick-time, yet he did it by maneuvering on tiptoe like Macmillan in the Common Market case (with just a touch of shot-gun like Macmillan in the Nassau case). When Wilson let Polaris reach the Cabinet for "decision," leading ministers, both "right" and "left," already were committed individually through things they had been led to say or do in one another's presence at informal working sessions. By that time also, Wilson had pre-tested back-bench sentiment, "prematurely" voicing to an acquiescent House what would become the rationale for Cabinet action: keeping on with weapons whose production had already passed a "point of no return." [5]

Superficially, such instances as these seem striking *un*presidential. In our accustomed vision, Presidents do not tiptoe around their Cabinets, they instruct, inform, or ignore them. They do not engineer *faits accomplis* to force decisions from them, for the Cabinet does not make decisions, *Presidents* decide. A Kennedy after Birmingham, a Johnson after Selma, deciding on their civil rights bills, or a Johnson after Pleiku, ordering the bombers north, or Johnson last December, taking off our pressure for the multilateral force, or Kennedy confronting Moscow over Cuba with advisers all around him but decisions in his hands—what contrasts these suggest with the maneuvers of a Wilson or Macmillan!

The contrasts are but heightened by a glance at their workforces: Presidents with twenty-odd high-powered personal assistants, and a thousand civil servants in their Executive Office—Prime Ministers with but four such assistants in their Private Office (three of them on detail from departments) and a handful more in the Cabinet Office, which by definition is not "theirs" alone. Differences of workplace heighten the effect still more: 10 Downing Street is literally a house, comparing rather poorly with the White House before T.R.'s time. The modern White House is a palace, as Denis Brogan keeps reminding us, a physically cramped version of the Hofburg, or the Tuileries.[6]

Yet beneath these contrasts, despite them, belying them, Americans are bound to glimpse a long-familiar pattern in the conduct of an activist Prime Minister. It is the pattern of a President maneuvering around or through the power-men in his Administration *and* in Congress. Once this is seen all contrasts become superficial. Underneath our images of Presidents-in-boots, astride decisions, are the half-observed realities of Presidents-in-sneakers, stirrups in hand, trying to induce particular department heads, or congressmen, or senators to climb aboard.

Anyone who has an independent power base is likelier than not to get "prime-ministerial" treatment from a President. Even his own appointees are to be wooed, not spurned, in the degree that they have their own attributes of power: expertise, or prestige, or a statute under foot. As Theodore Sorensen reported while he still was at the White House:

> In choosing between conflicting advice, the President is also choosing between conflicting advisers. . . . He will be slow to overrule a Cabinet officer whose pride or prestige has been committed, not only to save the officer's personal prestige but to maintain his utility. . . . Whenever any President overrules any Secretary he runs the risk of that Secretary grumbling, privately, if not publicly, to the Congress, or to the Press (or to his diary), or dragging his feet on implementation, or, at the very worst, resigning with a blast at the President.[7]

But it is men of Congress more than departmental men who regularly get from Pennsylvania Avenue the treatment given Cabinet ministers from Downing Street. Power in the Senate is particularly courted. A Lyndon Johnson when he served there, or a Vandenberg in Truman's time, or nowadays an Anderson, a Russell, even Mansfield, even Fulbright—to say nothing of Dirksen—are accorded many of the same attentions which a Wilson has to offer a George Brown.

The conventions of "bipartisanship" in foreign relations, established under Truman and sustained by Eisenhower, have been extended under Kennedy and Johnson to broad sectors of the home front, civil rights especially. These never were so much a matter of engaging oppositionists in

White House undertakings as of linking to the White House men from either party who had influence to spare. Mutuality of deference between Presidents and leaders of congressional opinion, rather than between the formal party leaderships, always has been of the essence to "bipartisanship" in practice. And men who really lead opinion on the Hill gain privileged access to Executive decisions as their customary share of "mutual deference." "Congress" may not participate in such decisions, but these men often do: witness Dirksen in the framing of our recent Civil Rights Acts, or a spectrum of Senators from Russell to Mansfield in the framing of particular approaches to Vietnam. Eleven years ago, Eisenhower seems to have kept our armed forces out of there when a projected intervention at the time of Dien Bien Phu won no support from Senate influentials. Johnson now maneuvers to maintain support from "right" to "left" within their ranks.

If one seeks our counterparts for Wilson or Macmillan as Cabinet tacticians one need look no farther than Kennedy or Johnson maneuvering among the influentials both downtown *and* on the Hill (and in state capitals, steel companies, trade unions, for that matter). Macmillan's caution on the Common Market will suggest the tortuous, slow course of JFK toward fundamental changes in our fiscal policy, which brought him only to the point of trying for a tax cut by the start of his fourth year. Macmillan's *fait accompli* on Polaris brings to mind the South-East Asian Resolution Johnson got from Congress after there had been some shooting in the Tonkin Gulf—and all its predecessors back to 1955 when Eisenhower pioneered this technique for extracting a "blank check." Wilson's quiet, quick arrangement for the Labour Party to adopt Polaris has a lot in common with the Johnson coup a year ago on aid to education, where a shift in rationale took all sorts of opponents off the hook.

British government may not be presidential but our government is more prime ministerial than we incline to think. Unhappily for thought, we too have something called a Cabinet. But that pallid institution is in no sense the equivalent of theirs. Our equivalent is rather an informal, shifting aggregation of key individuals, the influentials at both ends of Pennsylvania Avenue. Some of them may sit in what we call the Cabinet as department heads; others sit in back rows there, as senior White House aides; still others have no place there. Collectively these men share no responsibility nor any meeting ground. Individually, however, each is linked to all the others through the person of the President (supported by his telephone). And all to some degree are serviced—also monitored—by one group or another on the White House staff. The "Bundy Office," and the former "Sorensen Shop," which one might best describe now as the Moyers "sphere of influence," together with the staff of legislative liaisoners captained until lately by Lawrence O'Brien—these groups although not tightly interlocked provide a common reference point for influentials everywhere: "This is the White House calling. . . ." While we lack an institutionalized Cabinet along British lines, we are evolving an equivalent of the Cabinet Office. The O'Brien operation is its newest element, with no precursors worthy of the name in any regime earlier than Eisenhower's. Whether it survives, and how and why, without O'Brien become questions of the day for Presidency-watchers. Doctoral candidates take note!

The functional equivalence between a British Cabinet and our set of influentials—whether Secretaries, Senators, White House staffers, Congressmen, or others—is rendered plain by noting that for most intents and purposes their Cabinet members do the work of our congressional committees, our floor leaderships, and our front offices downtown, all combined. The combination makes for superficial smoothness; Whitehall seems a quiet place. But once again appearances deceive. Beneath the surface this combine called "Cabinet" wrestles with divergencies of interest, of perspective, of procedure, of personality, much like those we are used to witnessing above ground in the dealings of our separated institutions. Not only is the hidden struggle reminiscent of our open one, but also the results are often similar: "bold, new ventures" actually undertaken are often few and far between. Whitehall dispenses with the grunts and groans of Washington, but both can labor mightily to bring forth mice.

It is unfashionable just now to speak of "stalemate" or of "deadlock" in our government, although these terms were all the rage two years ago and will be so again, no doubt, whenever Johnson's coattails shrink. But British government is no less prone to deadlock than our own. Indeed I am inclined to think their tendencies in that direction more pronounced than ours. A keen observer of their system, veteran of some years at Cabinet meetings, put it to me in these terms:

> The obverse of our show of monolithic unity behind a Government position when we have one is slowness, ponderousness, deviousness, in approaching a position, getting it taken, getting a "sense of the meeting." Nothing in our system is harder to do, especially if press leaks are at risk. You Americans don't seem to understand that. . . .

In the Common Market case, to cite but one example, the three months from October to December 1962 were taken up at Brussels, where negotiations centered, by a virtual filibuster from the British delegation. This drove some of the Europeans wild and had them muttering about "perfidious Albion." But London's delegates were not engaged in tactical maneuvering at Brussels. All they were doing there was to buy time for tactical maneuvering back home, around the Cabinet table. The three months were required to induce two senior ministers to swallow agricultural concessions every student of the subject knew their government would have to make. But Britain could not move until those influential "members of the government" had choked them down. The time lag seemed enormous from the vantage point of Brussels. Significantly it seemed short indeed to Londoners. By Whitehall standards this was rapid motion.

One of the checks-and-balances in Britain's system lies between the PM and his colleagues as a group. This is the check that operated here. A sensible Prime Minister, attuned to his own power stakes, is scrupulous about the forms of collective action: overreaching risks rejection; a show of arbitrariness risks collegial reaction; if they should band together his associates could pull him down. Accordingly, the man who lives at Number 10 does well to avoid policy departures like the plague, unless, until, and if, he sees a reasonable prospect for obtaining that "sense of the meeting." He is not without resources to induce the prospect, and he is at liberty to ride events which suit his causes. But these things take time—and timing. A power-wise Prime Minster adjusts his pace accordingly. So Macmillan did in 1962.[8]

Ministerial prerogatives are not the only source of stalemate or slow motion in this system. If members of a Cabinet were not also heads of great departments, then the leader of their party in the Commons and the country might be less inclined to honor their pretensions in the government. A second, reinforcing check-and-balance of the system lies between him and the senior civil servants. To quote again, from the same source:

> The PM has it easier with ministers than with the civil servants. The ranks of civil servants do not work for him. They have to be brought along. They are loyal to a "Government Decision" but that takes the form of action in Cabinet, where the great machines are represented by their ministers.

The civil servants can be his allies, of course, if their perceptions of the public interest square with his and all he needs is to bring ministers along. Something of this sort seems to have been a factor in the Labour government's acceptance of Polaris: Foreign Office and Defence officials urged their masters on; Treasury officials remained neutral. The PM who first manages to tie the civil servants tighter to his office than to their own ministries will presidentialize the British system beyond anything our system knows. But that day is not yet. For obvious reasons it may never come.

So a British Premier facing Cabinet is in somewhat the position of our President confronting the Executive departments and Congress combined. Our man, compared to theirs, is freer to take initiatives and to announce them *in advance* of acquiescence from all sides. With us, indeed, initiatives in public are a step toward obtaining acquiescence, or at least toward wearing down the opposition. It is different in Downing Street. With us, also, the diplomatic and defense spheres yield our man authority for binding judgments on behalf of the whole government. Although he rarely gets unquestioning obedience and often pays a price, his personal choices are authoritative, for he himself is heir to royal prerogatives. In Britain these adhere to Cabinet members as a group, not the Prime Minister alone. Unless they stop him he can take over diplomacy, as Neville Chamberlain did so disastrously, and others since, or he even run a war like Winston Churchill. But Chamberlain had to change Foreign Secretaries in the process, and Churchill took precautions, making himself Minister of Defence.

Still, despite all differences, a President like a Prime Minister lives daily under the constraint that he must bring along *his* "colleagues" and get action from *their* liege-men at both ends of the Avenue. A sensible Prime Minister is always counting noses in Cabinet. A sensible President is always checking off his list of "influentials." The PM is not yet a President. The President, however, is a sort of super Prime Minister. This is what comes of comparative inquiry!

5

Later Reflections

When I first drafted what became "White House and Whitehall," Lyndon Johnson had succeeded JFK some seven months before, and was well on his way to legislative triumphs followed by a huge electoral victory. Macmillan had been gone nine months, resigning in the face of unexpected surgery, replaced by Home in an inactive mode, while Harold Wilson waited in the wings for his election.

At the time, I thought "White House and Whitehall" a fair characterization of the two governments and of long-lasting differences, as well as striking similarities, between them. I had no notion that I was capturing both systems at the tail end of a period of relative stability, about to be succeeded by continuing revolutions, still proceeding at the century's end, which would transform both profoundly—and show no signs of abating. No comparable comparison can be assayed today. Both systems are too much in motion.

Their motion reflects partly, but fundamentally, the continuing revolution in the means of mass communication, not least television, now the Internet besides. Partly it reflects successive events: In the United States those events obviously include Vietnam, then Watergate, eventually the end of the Cold War, and in between a generation of dissatisfactions with economic performance, set off by inflation, recession, stagnation, taxation, women in the workforce, and "downsizing," singly or combined. Along with these come striking changes in the flow of immigrants; fewer from Europe, many more from Latin America and Asia. Perhaps most striking is the rise of Republicans to dominance in what becomes a contested, two-party South.

Within the Republican Party itself this fuels the rise of the Christian right, and brings to power in congressional committees a different sort of southerner from the old-style agrarian, internationalist Southern Democrats.[1]

Britain has its economic counterparts, along with the definitive end of Empire, progressive loss of social deference, the "winter of discontent" in 1979, temporary capture of the Labour Party by the left, eleven years of Margaret Thatcher, and then Tory disarray, including public squabbles, under her successor—all feeding a decline of confidence in government, albeit rather less than in America, the home of antigovernment as ideology.[2]

For both countries, of course, there also is the march of generations, baby boomers in the van, which leaves the forty-somethings of the 1960s (to say nothing of their elders)—who remembered the Depression and had fought in World War II and seen the coming of the Welfare State, as well as the Cold War—now long-since retired, or dead.

Still, mass-communication changes remain at the root of continuing change in both machines of government. These are not of a piece, not all in one direction, so nothing observed today is necessarily predictive of tomorrow, nor is anything seen yesterday assuredly so now. Vietnam, for instance, is recalled in America as the first televised war, and pictures from those jungles, every night in living rooms, surely had effects on public tolerance for protracted struggle. But those were not live pictures. They were taken before minicameras, satellite transmission, and truly fast photographic development had come to pass. They do not compare for flexibility and timing, hence immediacy, with the shot of the light-haired Marine being dragged through the streets of Mogadishu in the fall of 1993. Had they done so, the demands to "win" the Vietnam war or quit—right now—might well have come much sooner and been drastically more intense. Had such pictures as that been available still earlier, in the Korean war, Truman, I suppose, would have been impeached.

For another instance of unstable consequences when technology and techniques in communications change, consider Ronald Reagan's exploitation of what television lent the White House early in his first term. That was still the heyday of the three traditional networks—ABC, CBS, and NBC—whose nightly news shows were named in polls as primary news sources by something over 80 percent of Americans. News was then seen as a crown jewel for each network, not a profit center, expense no bar. The Washington bureaus were lavishly run, the White House assignment prized, a significant step toward the top of electronic journalism. What made it so was its nearness to pictures of the President, almost always newsworthy in Cold War days, or at least of the building, known and symbolic to all—a relatively interesting backdrop for the journalist's talking head, provided that the White House as an organization gave her or him something to say.

Feeding the need of networks for such news and the ambition of reporters to provide it became a formidable weapon of news management in the hands of able White House aides, backed by a President who understood performing for a camera. To their "theme of the day," Reagan's people even managed to subordinate the President's own schedule, along with public appearances.

Moreover, the still-confident networks were then prepared to honor precedents which reached back to the days of FDR on radio. These allowed the President to "preempt" live network time, at his option, without charge, on at least two networks, whenever he had something he thought nationally important—outside the realm of party politics per se—to tell his national public. Most members of the public, then, had no choice but to listen to him, or to one other program, or turn off the set. In April 1981, when Reagan, in pajamas, recovering from an assassination attempt, chose to address the public in that fashion, appealing for his economic program before Congress, his audience was national indeed.[3]

Yet all that is now gone, swept away in the aftermath of cable and satellites. Traditional network news is now the primary news source for less than 50 percent of the country. Specialized news networks, local programs, radio at commuting times, compete to increasing effect. News even leaks around the edges in the form of casual references and opinions to make specialized programs of other sorts into "primary" sources for increasing numbers of people. Sports networks, as well as counterparts for civics, nature, arts, and movies, to say nothing of talk shows and their hosts, radio included, contribute mites of news, or what passes as such, which are apparently enough to meet the meager needs of many.

The traditional networks are now parts of larger commercial enterprises. Network news programs are now profit centers, perforce under increasing pressure. In the absence of sex, war, insurrection, bloody terrorism, or the next "big" California earthquake and the like, presidential "fireside chats," as Roosevelt called them, are unlikely to be granted free network TV time. In 1995, President Bill Clinton's requests for preemption were refused on at least two occasions.[4] To rouse public support for his side of the argument that winter, when his Republican congressional opponents threatened to close the federal government, Clinton had to resort to paid television ads, as though his quarrel with Congress were the same thing as political campaigning.

By paying TV stations all across the country, using funds that he and the

Vice President had hastily solicited from private sources, Clinton reached and favorably impressed, so it is said, a national audience, which stood him in good stead when he faced down Congress.[5]

Titillating sex aside, this may have been the only way that Clinton (and his successors?) could have sought or hoped to find a helpful national public. Short of the encompassing emergency, or scandal, and apart from that annual civics lesson, the State of the Union Message, free television time no longer is the source of such a thing. On the contrary, cable and satellites, now joined by the Internet, produce "narrowcasting" effects, which chip "the" public into disconnected segments.

All this has happened less than a generation after TV network news so strengthened Reagan. The contrast may owe something to the human and political dimensions of two Presidents. But it owes more to technology, along with managerial adjustments. What comes next?

An American President still confronts, just as in the 1960s, an essentially prime-ministerial task. He needs to persuade a sufficiency of influentials, in Congress and out (rather than in Cabinet), to do what he wants done, so that there is a likelihood that it will come to pass, then be sustained. For this he is less well equipped than formerly. The absence of the Cold War makes his wishes seem to matter less in almost every sphere. And the decline of an assured national public makes him less able than ever to appeal beyond those influentials to the particular publics on which they depend.

Clinton indeed did manage it, despite himself, in the Lewinsky case, but that had best be seen as an exception to prove the rule.

Paradoxically, the influentials on Capitol Hill seem individually stronger in themselves, yet weaker in their capacity to deal with and deliver one another—so less able to bargain conclusively with a President. On the one hand, they have massive professional staffs, some ten times the size of those in 1964. They have unprecedented access to TV, including what matters most, their local stations. They also run their own campaigns for nomination and election, with little or no help from the national party. They mostly raise their own campaign funds. Once elected, members of Congress still bargain with their party chiefs for committee assignments, but no longer do they keep their mouths shut through their first decade, nor do they have to wait long for a subcommittee chair, with its attendant privileges and aides.

On the other hand, most politicians find fund-raising an inordinate chore, which paid TV ads and political-consultant fees—the top two items of expense—make very burdensome. They then have to yield access to campaign contributors, along with well-staffed interest groups and well-intentioned voters from back home who can afford jet fares to Washington, as all too many can. (Judging from Clinton, Presidents are now in the same situation.) Moreover, scarcely any members of the House and Senate any longer think they hold safe seats for either nomination or election. All are haunted by the specter, if not prospect, of the rich contender parachuting in, on his or her impulse, with his or her own money—which the Supreme Court has ruled can be spent without stint.

Influentials of that sort have independence from each other, as well as from the President. Partisan alignments in congressional votes have rarely been higher than now, but that speaks less to party discipline by leaders than to similarities in the hot breaths which local activists, interests, and funders, in primaries all across the country, puff on the necks of candidates bearing the same party label—especially now that the South is contested too. The congressional party chiefs, both committee and floor leaders, can rarely commit their followers except by estimating where they mean to go anyway, and such estimates are often wrong. To a degree this was true in 1964, but seems much more so now. And by comparison with 1934, or 1904, the contrast is great indeed.

As for influentials outside Congress, only four Cabinet members count for much with Presidents from day to day: State, Treasury, Defense, and Justice. Occasionally, one or more of these are quasi-independent by virtue of their press or public following. Rarely, however, can they deliver each other, to say nothing of anybody else. State governors draw further from the White House as federal flows of funds decrease. They, too, are rarely able to deliver one another. There remain the persons in the private sector, legions of them, with clout over decisions in social or economic spheres which a President may find he needs to borrow—running all the way from Wall Streeters to baseball players, with moguls of the media and many sorts of others in between. Their cases vary, perhaps no more now than a generation ago, but their capacity to influence each other, on the President's say-so, surely seems diminished as compared with World War II, or even Kennedy's term.

What of the federal bureaucracy? The military chiefs still can do as they always could, and did—play "their" congressional committees or indebted leaders off against the President. The White House staff and associated aides, five or six times as many as in 1962, are relatively loyal, but sometimes too much so, more royalist than the king. And as political appointees they are but birds of passage, the least permanent people in town. As for the career civil servants, they are removed from the presidency by far thicker layers than formerly of appointive officials, hundreds more than in the 1960s, and are surrounded by far more organized interests, together with intently micromanaging congressional committee staffs.

Protection for "their" programs makes the better civil servants no less passionate than before, but it is a passion more than ever divorced from the White House, pursued without the contacts of an Owen or a Schaetzel, by successors who have taken such a beating from their masters in successive administrations that they mostly lack the confidence as well. The civil services in general and the Foreign Service in particular seem weaker than before, in stamina and also in talent. But they still do the work without which little else gets done. They still have advice of importance to weigh. They still can resist, and they do. From a President's perspective there are still influentials among them.

The country, in short, is crammed with "influentials," but from a White House standpoint they are mostly individual entrepreneurs, carrying their own baggage, seeking their own sustenance, feeling little group loyalty and less group pressure—hard indeed to bargain with, for any lasting effect.

The "President in sneakers" I envisaged in "White House and Whitehall" wears something more like scruffy sandals now, while those he asks to ride his horse are liable to fall off at the next bounce. If, in 1964, he seemed more "prime ministerial" than "presidential" as traditionally conceived, he now seems institutionally weaker than any British Premier in memory, save that fictional PM of Anthony Trollope's imagination, Plantagenet Palliser (comparing assured influence, not temperament!).

The British have not seen so weakly placed a chief executive as the American now seems to be since, perhaps, late Stuart times. Tony Blair professes to admire Bill Clinton. The reality is that Clinton has every reason to envy Blair.

For the British counterparts to forces and events that push our Presidency down have pushed their Premiership up, to heights beyond the reckoning of even a Macmillan. Blair, as a successor to Thatcher, and a smoother article by far than she, is the most "presidential" character on either side of the Atlantic since the early Ronald Reagan in popular appeal and the early Lyndon Johnson in parliamentary product.

Changes in the media have not been the same in the United Kingdom as in the United States. In a far smaller geographic space, cable is not yet a big deal, satellite dishes are still not the norm, and while five TV channels replace the two of the BBC's one-time monopoly, narrowcasting in the American sense does not exist to anything like the same degree. TV news and commentary and panel shows all remain central to the coverage of government. Moreover, radio has never ceased to be important as a source of news, and newspapers remain so, both the broadsheets and the tabloids in their respective ways. These, indeed, have always purveyed a form of narrowcasting-in-print, and still do. But print, even in tabloid form, is generically different from live pictures.

What has changed, in the main, is reporting, print as well as electronic (which means alteration also in the expectations of editors, readers, viewers, and listeners). British journalists no longer keep a safe distance from Whitehall—safe, that is, from the government's standpoint. No longer do they tamely crowd the lobby of the House of Commons, or report at length on the proceedings there. Debates are rarely covered save in snippets featuring sound bites. Rather, the reporters pursue ministers and noteworthy MPs, or anybody else of interest, to their lairs, bearding them in offices, or grassy plots, or restaurants, and demanding their reactions not only to the scandals but also to the policy disputes or departures of the day. Emphasis is on the personalities, rather than on the grayer stuff of policy and process. In that respect the journalists of London outdo even those in Washington.

And Members of the House of Commons, rising to their feet, trade sound bites now, not speeches, for the one might get them on the TV news and radio, while the other will rarely be printed.[6]

At election time, the journalists and photographers swarm around frontbenchers of the national parties. They follow the Prime Minister and opposition counterparts wherever they campaign, with far less notice for constituency candidates whose personal elections are, ostensibly, the object of it all. The parties play up to this, with advertisements and telecasts emphasizing national, not local themes, and also national personalities. By common consent those are the parliamentary leaders, the PM and his institutional opponents above all. The influence of television is, of course, pervasive. So, in recent campaigns, is that of American consultants and techniques. All put the emphasis upon 10 Downing Street and its next incumbent, quite as though it were the White House and he or she the President. Increasingly, in fact, he or she is.

Not only changes in communication but the conduct of the office is responsible for this. It is the product, in large part, of Margaret Thatcher's doings in her lengthy Premiership and of the precedents then set, on which her successors can build if they so choose—as John Major did not but as Blair obviously does. (Not every successor will choose in Blair's way; there are bound to be other John Majors.)

Many of the things that in Macmillan's time were taken to be almost constitutional, as limits on the ways in which a government did business, were ignored or changed by Thatcher. She was trying nothing less than to transform key attitudes in her society, transforming for the purpose her own party, and her means to do both lay in reaching for more personal control of the Whitehall machine. Government decisions, binding on civil servants as well as ministers, no longer required a sense-of-the-meeting by the whole Cabinet, recorded in Cabinet minutes. Rather, they were taken, for the most part, in rump meetings between the PM and the ministers she chose to bring together, recorded by such minutes as she chose to sanction. Ministers were cautioned, preempted, or turned around on decisions taken even in their own departments. Government information offices were politicized. A policy unit at Number 10—originating in Wilson's time, augmented in Heath's, more so in Thatcher's—patrolled their jurisdictions. So, of course, did the Cabinet Office, which became more nearly the PM's own staff than ever before.

And the once self-managing civil service had to adjust to active intervention from above in choosing permanent heads of department. Not political conformity, exactly, but rather intellectual sympathy, temperamental affinity—"one of us"—was what Thatcher wanted from her mandarins. Increasingly, she got it.[7]

By the same token, she and her ministers increasingly insisted that the task of civil servants was to implement what they proposed, not contest it. The traditional right of officials to put policies forward and argue for them to the bitter end, conceding only when ministers actually chose otherwise, was frowned on in the Thatcher years. This was carried to the point that senior civil servants eventually ceased claiming it, settling instead for the lesser right to work out just how implementing ministerial initiatives was to be managed.[8]

Where does all this leave the "tacit treaty" between politicians and officials, so emphasized in Chapter 4 as of the early 1960s? On the ministerial side it seems still more or less intact—although the numbers of political appointees in private offices increase—but on the civil service side the treaty is distinctly tattered. No longer is it so rewarding to become the servants of Her Majesty. Not only is there less prospective power over policy, there also is less social honor, less immunity from Parliament, and—horrors—less assured insulation from the press. (The same can be said for the Queen, of course, not to speak of the heir to the throne, which is part of the servants' problem.)

As early as 1965, in Harold Wilson's first Administration, civil service knighthoods were reduced in number. Wilson was also creator of what, under Thatcher, evolved into continuing select committees in the House of Commons, parallel to Whitehall's departments. Those committees play no direct part in legislating, and are largely nonpartisan in conduct, as in composition, but they do review departmental performance, including that of civil servants. Over the years, this system began to be real. Coupled to the ministerial affinity for journalists, an inevitable, continuing phenomenon, and the latter's current lack of deference toward government, that emergent reality becomes threatening. When scandals erupt from departmental doings, whether in weapons sales, or defense procurement, or prison management—all recent instances—or anything else, what security have civil servants, nowadays, that they can remain anonymous, that they rarely need testify, that ministers will always take the rap? Subjectively, at least, the answers are not reassuring.

Uncertainty about the old convention of ministerial responsibility is heightened by the fact that, both in Thatcher's years and since, the departments have been spinning off into autonomy a multitude of operating functions. Sometimes these have gone into quasi-independent entities ("Quangoes"), something like our Post Office, more often into separate though subordinate agencies, approximating the U.S. Park Service, or Forest Service, or the Bureau of Standards and the like, each with its administrator heading its own career system. Is the parent department's minister responsible to Parliament for what these do or don't? Where does the department "head" come in, the Permanent Secretary? Answers will evolve with practice but just now seem far from settled. That adds to insecurity among the civil servants.

Their insecurity seems rational to me. If ever journalists and editors on their own motion decide that mandarins are newsworthy and photogenic, nothing in the stance of ministers since Thatcher's time suggests that they will bar the way to journalistic exploitation of officials. Their immunity, I think, will come to a crashing end. The "tacit treaty" could not long survive.

If Tony Blair, as Thatcher's heir, is presidential now, the present situation has potential for becoming positively Washingtonian.

One thing, however, may prevent it. Mrs. Thatcher overstepped the boundaries of nonarbitrariness in form, due process in appearance, which Macmillan in the Skybolt case preserved as of the essence of collective responsibility. That is the characteristic of British Cabinet government which fundamentally distinguishes it from presidential government in the United States. Ultimately, overstepping brought Thatcher down. When back-bench rebellion threatened, spurred by electoral fears, her Cabinet colleagues did not rally to her cause. Instead they mostly lined up with three "big beasts of the Jungle," in the Tory phrase—figures of great party weight and national prestige—whom she had previously, incautiously, thrown out of Cabinet, one by one, onto the back bench where they were free to fan revolt and did.[9] Whereupon her Cabinet colleagues told her she could not win reelection to the parliamentary party leadership, and hence should go before she was thus pushed—at which she went.

Blair shows every sign of knowing that he has to treat his big beasts carefully, and even smaller ones with some semblance of courtesy. (Thatcher too knew better in her early years.) The biggest are all in his Cabinet now and indeed serve with him on a sort of executive committee. Presumably he will not pull apart that collectivity or its successors to such a point that he destroys his base as primus-inter-pares. For he lacks an electoral base of his own, and even television, I surmise, cannot quite give it to him.

A Prime Minister's principal formal power is not only that he chooses all the ministers but also that he personally decides the date, hence fate, of everyone's election. Yet balancing that, ultimately, those ministers, reflecting party sentiment in Commons, still can unseat the PM, even as they did Thatcher. So Macmillan's concern for collective colleagueship was prudent, even if, by her standards, old-fashioned. Blair had best not forget, despite the media focus on him.

The contrast with American Presidents in their fixed terms is sharp, at least before the dire precedent of Nixon's resignation—which now tempts both the media and Congress to play "gotcha" against his successors.

If prime-ministerial behavior in coming years somehow preserves the colleagueship of Cabinet, even while dispensing with traditional decision-making methods, there will be something for the collectivity of civil servants to relate to. An amended treaty may evolve. Governing in London then would not be tantamount to the still-passionate warfare of Washington. But I think it can never again be the comfortable duopoly that it once was. The media, and after them the NGOs—indeed to some extent still wider publics—have their feet too firmly planted in the door. And I presume the means of mass communication, still being revolutionized, will force it further open, year by year.

Acknowledgments

When my Skybolt report was declassified in 1993, I asked the Kennedy School Case Program at Harvard University to issue it as a "case" in its series. I gratefully acknowledge the Case Program's prompt response, which made the report readily available to researchers, as well as to interested instructors of courses in foreign policy and international relations. One of those instructors, Robert Jervis of Columbia University, found the report so useful in his teaching that he first urged, then facilitated publication with institutional context added: in brief, this book. Now that the book's finished, I can thank him for that without qualification, and can withdraw the "case," which I have done. Another user who cheered me on was Philip Zelikow, then a Harvard colleague, now Director of the Miller Center at the University of Virginia.

Three others did me the great favor of critically commenting on drafts for the new chapters. They are Anthony King of the University of Essex, Ernest R. May of Harvard, both long-suffering old friends, and my wife, Shirley Williams, simultaneously of Harvard and the British House of Lords. I thank them for their critical comments, most of which I heeded, but I retain responsibility for all mistakes. Shirley deserves gratitude, as well, for tolerating without complaint my absences from home while I was holed up on Cape Cod, writing. And my Harvard assistant, Sally Makacynas, is owed thanks for effective performance of many chores, not least fending off the press during the Monica Lewinsky madness. Also, I am grateful to Cornell University Press for making our relationship as painless and pleasant as such things can be.

Finally, I am forever indebted to the person who commissioned my study and read my report, John F. Kennedy—that rarity in Presidents of the United States, someone detached enough yet confident enough to truly seek to learn from experience.

RICHARD E. NEUSTADT

Wellfleet, Massachusetts
November 1998

Notes

1. Introduction

1. The report was declassified April 15, 1992.

2. It was my custom to take almost no notes during an interview—lest this distract the other person—then, as soon as possible afterward, to regurgitate everything onto a pad in pen-and-ink. Several of those handwritten notes I cannot now locate. Many, however, are in the papers I deposited at the Kennedy Library in 1978, See Boxes 19 and 19A, under "Memos of Conversation" and "Europe—MLF/Skybolt," folder 2, with numerous withdrawals on account of security classification. Those withdrawals are under review at my request. It is conceivable that the missing items will turn up among them.

For the Skybolt report, I translated my scrawls into finished memoranda of conversation whenever I planned to quote someone at length, just in case the President should ask about the context. This means that on the American side I did not do so for dozens of conversations with other officials, too many to recall. On the British side, where my interviewing was more selective, I can particularize, albeit from memory. I did interview but did not create memcons for at least the following: Reginald Maudling, the Chancellor, Norman McLeod, the Conservative Leader of the Commons and recent Colonial Secretary, Will Hawthorne, the MOD adviser, and on the Labour side, not yet in office, George Brown (then Labour Foreign Affairs spokesman), Denis Healey, Roy Jenkins, and Harold Wilson, soon to be respectively, the Secretaries of State for Economic Affairs and for Defence, the Minister of Aviation, and the Prime Minister. Hugh Gaitskell, the Labour Party leader in 1962, whose opposition to British entry into EEC and scorn for Skybolt were both fierce, had unexpectedly died in January 1963 and thus was off my list.

The interview notes that were turned into memcons which will be available through the Kennedy Library are identified as follows, with dates (all 1963 except where otherwise noted): *Americans*: George Ball, May 24 and July 2; David Bell, June 20; Charles Bohlen, July 16; Robert Bowie, July 1; McGeorge Bundy, May 28; JFK, April 27; Carl Kaysen, June 1; Robert McNamara, May 30, June 29, and April 11, 1964; Livingston Merchant, June 28; Paul Nitze, June 19; Henry Owen, May 25; Walt Rostow, May 23; Henry Rowen,

June 14 and July 1; Dean Rusk, May 28 and August 27; Theodore Sorensen, May 24; General Maxwell Taylor, July 3; William Tyler, June 1 and June 14; Seymour Weiss, May 29; and Adam Yarmolinsky, June 12, June 13, and June 19. *British*: Timothy Bligh, July 31 and August 1; Michael Butler (British Embassy, Paris), July 15; Michael Cary, son of the novelist Joyce Cary, July 30; Philip de Zulueta, August 2 and August 16; Arthur Hockaday, August 2; Edward Heath, July 26; David Ormsby Gore, June 18; Peter Thorneycroft, July 30; and Solly Zuckerman, July 12.

3. By telegram on July 15, 1963, responding to an inquiry from Sir Robert Scott, the Permanent Secretary of the MOD (who had advance word of my trip from Alastair Buchan, a mutual friend), Ormsby Gore confirmed Buchan's description of me and my purpose, then added "I did not feel sure of the constitutional propriety of questioning British Ministers in order to provide a personal report to the President of the United States. . . . This is a point which can only be decided in London" (UK Public Record Office file, PREM 11/4737).

3. British Refinements

1. U.K. Public Record Office, PREM 11/4737, July 30, 1963.

2. The files of the Cabinet Office, PM's Private Office. Foreign Office, MOD, and Royal Air Force for 1960–63 have been consulted, also the Admiralty files for 1960–61 (the counterpart for 1963 remains classified and that for 1962 has not been located). All these are at the Public Record Office, Kew Gardens, London, and are identified by reference number as appropriate, in notes below. There are, of course, many duplications of documents. With regard to each, I cite the file in which I first happened to find it.

3. AIR 19/1036, Thorneycroft to Macmillan, undated, December 1962.

4. All in PREM 11/3716, indicated dates.

5. CAB 139/189 Gen 778, November 29, 1962.

6. DEFE 13/410, "draft" but evidently sent, Thorneycroft to Macmillan, December 7, 1962.

7. Interview, May 30, 1963.

8. See, especially, the excellent history (from 1957 through 1962) by Ian Clark, *Nuclear Diplomacy and the Special Relationship* (London: Oxford University Press, 1994); see also Dominic Wilson's unpublished honors thesis, Merton College, Oxford, 1995.

9. Interview, July 30, 1963.

10. Interviews, July 31, August 1, 16, 1963.

11. AIR 19/1036, Hockaday to de Zulueta et al., November 9, 1962.

12. The law changed after Watergate, but until then the White House files were the President's personal property and left office with him, to be disposed of as he chose. FDR established the precedent of putting them in a privately built Library, so called, and giving both to the National Archives. Eisenhower did the same, but his Library at Abilene, Kansas, was not ready in 1963, so the files were in temporary storage near his Pennsylvania retirement residence.

13. For text see AIR 19/1036 or PREM 11/3716, November 9, 1962.

14. Interview, July 30, 1963.

15. PREM 11/3716, November 18, 1962, tel. 2891.

16. PREM 11/4229, Gore to Home, December 8, 1962, "to PM Dec 12."

17. PREM 11/3716, Thorneycroft to Home, November 8, 1962.

18. PREM 11/3716, Macmillan to de Zulueta, December 12, 1962.

19. AIR 19/1036, Fraser to Thorneycroft, October 16, 1962; see also, for flavor, CAS 3234 re Sir Solly Zuckerman.

20. AIR 19/1036, Fraser to Thorneycroft, November 11, 1962.

21. 2PREM 11/3716, Fraser to Thorneycroft, November 14, 1962.

22. DEFE 13/410, Fraser to Thorneycroft, November 29, 1962.

23. AIR 19/1036, Fraser to Thorneycroft, undated, December 1962.

24. 2AIR 19/1036, undated, December 1962.

25. PREM 11/4229, Gore to Home (for PM) December 14, 1962.

26. Interview, May 29, 1963. This is a matter of memory. My records show that a memcon was made of that interview, but it is missing from the file now to go to the Kennedy Library.

27. PREM 11/4229, Bligh for Butler, First Sec. State, "as from PM," December 20, 1962.

28. PREM 11/4229, Thorneycroft to Macmillan, December 19, 1962.

29. PREM 11/8716, prelim. papers for Cabinet committee guidelines, February–April 1962.

30. PREM 11/8716, Minute of PM interview with US SecDef., April 29, 1962.

31. See Ernest R. May and Philip D. Zelikow, eds., *The Kennedy Tapes* (Cambridge: Harvard University Press, 1997).

4. White House and Whitehall

1. See for an example of a "frank" political memoir, Hugh Dalton, *Memoirs*, 2: *High Tide and After* (London: Muller, 1962). For an example on the civil service side see Edward, Lord Bridges, *The Treasury*, New Whitehall Series no. 12 (London: Allen & Unwin, 1964).

2. I suggested at least a partial answer in "Politicians and Bureaucrats," *The Congress and America's Future* (New York: Prentice-Hall, 1965), pp. 115–16.

3. Regarding civil servants of an earlier era, when aristocratic patronage opened the way to careers, it is delightful to note that Sir Charles Trevelyan, one of the creators of the modern civil service, was accustomed to "sound off" on issues of the day, with which he was concerned as an official of the Treasury, in letters to the press. See Cecil Woodham-Smith, *The Great Hunger* (New York: Harper, 1962).

Regarding the military, I am indebted to Hugh Gaitskell, in a conversation in 1961, for the observation that the Opposition was the target of confidential griping from senior service officers to a degree "absolutely unknown" on the civilian side, "perhaps for the reason that the army and navy are so much older than the civil service and quite a lot older than Cabinet government. This gives a certain confidence. . . . They still rather regard themselves as 'servants of the crown,' *apart* from the government. The civil servants wouldn't dare; theirs is a 'junior' service . . . under Cabinet from the start."

4. There is some question whether the diet of a Private Secretary is not altogether too rich for a man on his way up civil service ladders in the rather special case of the Prime Minister's Private Office. Macmillan's Private Secretaries, both from the Treasury and from the Foreign Office, went not up but out. They had been too intimately and confidentially involved with too much power to resume the civil servant's climb within the ranks. I once speculated publicly that this might be the usual result, henceforth, given the heady atmosphere of Number 10 (*Sunday Times*, November 8, 1964, p. 41). This speculation drew a wager from the current PPS to the PM that *he*, unlike his predecessor, would be prepared to go back in and climb. When the time comes we shall see who wins that bet. [He won, in a way: leaving prematurely for a senior departmental post on the periphery of Downing Street's concerns, pushed by one of the PM's closest political aides, who was said to have forced a choice, "him or me."]

5. From the Prime Minister's statement to the House of Commons, defense debate, November 23, 1964.

6. Sir Denis Brogan, "The Presidency," in *American Aspects* (London: Hamish Hamilton, 1964), pp. 5–6.

7. Theodore Sorensen, *Decision-Making in the White House* (New York: Columbia University Press, 1963), pp. 79–80.

8. A man who seems to have made every mistake in the book on these scores, among others, is Anthony Eden, before, during, and after the Suez invasion of 1956.

5. Later Reflections

1. For a more extensive summary see my chapter, "The Politics of Public Mistrust," in Joseph S. Nye Jr. et al., eds., *Why People Don't Trust Government* (Cambridge: Harvard University Press, 1997). See also, in the same book, David C. King, "The Polarization of American Parties and Mistrust of Government."

2. For detail on the complex economic, social, and political reactions of the British to ruinous victory in World War II, possible sources are immensely wide and varied. The following four books, each covering specialized aspects and periods, collectively come close, I hope, to embodying the whole: Alistair Horne, *Macmillan, 1957–1986* (London: Macmillan, 1989); Ivor Crewe and Anthony King, *SDP: The Birth, Life, and Death of the Social Democratic Party* (Oxford: Oxford University Press, 1995); Philip Stephens, *Politics and the Pound* (London: Macmillan, 1996); and Hugo Young, *This Blessed Plot: Britain and Europe from Churchill to Blair* (London: Macmillan, 1998).

3. Reagan spoke live on two networks, April 28, 1981, to an estimated audience then thought exceptionally large according to press reports. Unfortunately, it had no Nielsen ratings, so those reports cannot be checked.

4. As told me by George Stephanopoulos in early 1996.

5. Dick Morris, *Behind the Oval Office* (New York: Random House, 1997), esp. pp. 138–57. Given circumstances of Reagan's sort in early 1981, I do not doubt that Clinton's successor still could preempt live network time. But this requires, first of all, near-death on television at the hands of a would-be assassin, preferably of a new President in his congressional honeymoon phase. Comparable emergencies can be envisaged. My point is, merely, that preemption will come hard without them.

6. Lord Jenkins of Hillhead, the former Home Secretary and Chancellor of the Exchequer, among many other things, writes authoritatively about the change in style and quality of House debate between the 1960s and the 1980s, and, insightfully, on his own incapacity to adapt. See Roy Jenkins, *Life at the Center* (New York: Random House, 1991).

7. For an extensive review of these matters see Hugo Young, *One of Us* (New York: Random House, 1996). For a comparatively brief but insightful commentary from a political scientist's standpoint, see Anthony King, "Margaret Thatcher as Political Leader," a paper prepared for delivery at the 1989 Annual Meeting of the American Political Science Association.

8. As best I understood them, this was the burden of the song of several very senior civil servants from a variety of ministries who spoke informally, under Chatham House rules, at a series of faculty dinners and teas in the University of Essex, while I was a visiting professor there during the mid-1990s.

9. The three were Michael Heseltine, Geoffrey Howe, and Nigel Lawson, respectively former President of the Board of Trade, Foreign Secretary, and Chancellor of the Exchequer.

Index